Looking Good Naked

Looking Good Naked

Youth Work and the Body of Christ

Andy du Feu

RESOURCE *Publications* • Eugene, Oregon

LOOKING GOOD NAKED
Youth Work and the Body of Christ

Copyright © 2020 Andy du Feu. All rights reserved. Except for brief quotations in critical publications or reviews, no part of this book may be reproduced in any manner without prior written permission from the publisher. Write: Permissions, Wipf and Stock Publishers, 199 W. 8th Ave., Suite 3, Eugene, OR 97401.

Resource Publications
An Imprint of Wipf and Stock Publishers
199 W. 8th Ave., Suite 3
Eugene, OR 97401

www.wipfandstock.com

PAPERBACK ISBN: 978-1-7252-5183-0
HARDCOVER ISBN: 978-1-7252-5184-7
EBOOK ISBN: 978-1-7252-5185-4

Manufactured in the U.S.A.   December 9, 2019

All Scripture quotations, unless otherwise indicated, are taken from the Holy Bible, New International Version®, NIV®. Copyright ©1973, 1978, 1984, 2011 by Biblica, Inc.™ Used by permission of Zondervan. All rights reserved worldwide. www.zondervan.com The "NIV" and "New International Version" are trademarks registered in the United States Patent and Trademark Office by Biblica, Inc.™

"Scripture quotations marked (ESV) are from The ESV® Bible (The Holy Bible, English Standard Version®), copyright © 2001 by Crossway, a publishing ministry of Good News Publishers. Used by permission. All rights reserved."

'Scriptures quoted marked (GNB) or 'Good News Bible' are from the Good News Bible © 1994 published by the Bible Societies/HarperCollins Publishers Ltd UK, Good News Bible© American Bible Society 1966, 1971, 1976, 1992. Used with permission.'

Scripture quotations marked (NLT) are taken from the Holy Bible, New Living Translation, copyright © 1996, 2004, 2007, 2013, 2015 by Tyndale House Foundation. Used by permission of Tyndale House Publishers, Inc., Carol Stream, Illinois 60188. All rights reserved.

"Scripture quotations marked (NASB) taken from the NEW AMERICAN STANDARD BIBLE®, Copyright © 1960,1962,1963,1968,1971,1972,1973,1975,1977,1995 by The Lockman Foundation. Used by permission."

Contents

List of Illustrations and Tables | vii

Foreword by Ron Belsterling | ix

Preface | xi

Acknowledgements | xvii

1. Don't forget to floss | 1
   Why we need a robust ecclesiology

2. False Expectations | 18
   Why we need clarity about people and roles

3. Mirrors = friends | 30
   Why self-reflection is so essential

4. Zombies are Biblical | 45
   How to start from scratch

5. Airbrushed youth ministry | 64
   How to put together a theologically rich dream team

6. Beyond the nip and tuck | 78
   How to develop a healthy body image

7. Let them go | 94
   Why we need voluntary communities

8. Fill them up | 100
   Why we need empowering communities

9. Clear their path | 108
   Why we need welcoming communities

10   Value them | 114
     Why we need time-rich communities

11   Hitting the city streets | 124
     How to be confident about church

Appendix 1: At what age in the UK? | 135

Appendix 2: David's Mighty Men (the Gibborim) | 137

Bibliography | 141

List of Illustrations and Tables

Figure 01: Young Head on Old Shoulders | 4

Figure 02: Ceremonial Value by Age and Gender in Shekels of Silver (Leviticus 27:1-8) | 5

Figure 03: La Corbière | 9

Figure 04: Cross Tides in Youth Work | 13

Figure 05: Superheroes Need Not Apply | 19

Figure 06: Johari Window | 36

Figure 07: STOP Before you Start: Towards an Applied Theology | 42

Figure 08: The S-Curve | 59

Figure 09: Hacking the S-Curve | 61

Figure 10: Riding the S-Wave | 62

Figure 11: Employment Selection Matrix | 71

Figure 12: #thehandshake | 72

Figure 13: Volunteer Vs Disciple | 76

Figure 14: Belbin's Team Roles | 81

Figure 15: Forward Spider-Web Chart | 86

Figure 16: "Total Football" Forward Spider-Web | 87

List of Illustrations and Tables

Figure 17: Focused Development Forward Spider-Web Chart | 88

Figure 18: Ladder of Participation | 101

Figure 19: Youth Voice Rubric | 103

Figure 20: Youth-Led Service Plan | 104

Figure 21: Limits to Empowerment | 105

Figure 22: Religious Affiliation by Decade of Birth, 1981-2011 | 126

Figure 23: Gough's Biblical Model for Youth Work | 130

Foreword

ANDY DU FEU AND I first met almost 20 years ago. Ironically, we did not meet while he lived and worked in Camden, N.J. and I lived in Haddonfield, N.J. (neighboring cities). We met later, in the U.K. By God's blessings, we have been able to stay in touch and minister together at times through these 20 years. Reading this book has reminded me of what I've known about Andy for a long time.

He has always impressed me as a man who cared deeply about youth ministry, his own disciples especially, and his extending communities as well. In conversations and by watching him minister in multiple contexts, he demonstrated deeper level thinking, practical intentionality, and contextual sensitivity. His wit and humor and energy naturally compel others toward him. He not only has a desire to teach and reach his mates, but he has also experienced much obvious success. As his family has grown, he has shown a passion to not sacrifice them for the sake of all of his other goals. All of those qualities and passions are on display in this book.

In *"Looking Good Naked"* Andy makes clear that he desires those in youth work to pursue true ministry to teenagers, worrying less about how we look in ministry and more about the impact we can have through the strengths and weaknesses we've been gifted with. He believes that if each youth worker understands his or her purpose and crafts a plan to see one's "vision come to life", that that person's efforts will prove effective. And quite possibly, more through our weaknesses than our strengths. He dives deeply into history, missiology, culture, social policy, and theology (the Bible and certain theologians) to weave together a book filled with insight, challenge, and encouragement. The inclusion of many stories illustrates and carries many of the points made.

Honestly, I'm actually jealous. With great wit, Andy writes a book which adeptly make his readers laugh, learn, think, cry, and strategize all

Foreword

the way through it. What is remarkable is that readers should be able finish it fairly quickly as well. This is because while its informative, it's interesting, enjoyable, and to the point. I'm fascinated that someone knows as much as he does, conversing as competently and fluidly with theologians like Moltmann, Grenz, and Root as with comic book heroes like Batman and Captain America.

The foundation of the book is clearly steeped in scripture. His study and intent on showing its practicality shine throughout the text. I feel like I learned much about passages that I had explored often before. It is refreshing to see a ministry book so relevant and reverent at the same time. I believe this to be the essential strength of the text.

Another realistic key strength of the book will be the practical companion it will be for many in youth work. Andy provides plenty of challenges and discussion questions in every chapter. All are creatively designed to challenge youth workers to deeper level thinking and practical implementation. While "discussion questions" or "ideas" might show up at the ends of chapters in many ministry books, there is nothing ordinary about Andy's questions. All of his wit and humor and study are as much on display in his questions as they are in the essential content of each chapter.

Two more points—Andy seems as sensitive to the plight and challenges of the volunteer as he is to the paid professional. Thus, volunteers will enjoy a book that helps them go beyond just the quick-fix-practical meeting guide, but not demand that they be available full time to execute some overwhelming ideas. Lastly, the beautiful aspect of this text will be its use to those in youth ministry in both the U.K. and in the U.S. Andy balances his examples and challenges and understanding of both cultures fairly equally, certainly making clear that he has ministry experience and insight in both sides of the world. Readers on both sides of the ocean will find much to relate to and much that will expand their thinking (and vocabulary).

Just reading *Looking Good Naked* and writing this Foreword already has generated some ideas as to how I can bring Andy's insights into the world of my students and colleagues. I want to do this because I know their global awareness and present work will benefit. And I'm confident that after reading this book, yours will too.

—Ron Belsterling
   Professor of Church & Ministry Leadership and Program Director of Youth & Young Adult Ministries for Lancaster Bible College & Capital Seminary.

Preface

I LOVE WORKING WITH young people. It's a place where paradox abounds. On the surface, it appears that an engaging personality and great soft skills outweigh anything learned in the classroom, and interactions occupy a precarious liminality, where you know one positive choice could open up incredible possibilities, even when the young person feels as though they are staring into the abyss. These are true regardless of context: whether face-to-face or training others, under the auspices of state or church, as friend or advocate, in rural village or inner city.

I love church, with all of her beautiful features and blemishes, successes and failings, proclamations and debates, expressions and complications.

Common to both is a profound sense of promise for the future, and the sense in which normal people like you and me get to play a creative role in shaping it. For all of the negatives that are heard and experienced, I cannot get away from the excitement of being involved in something so much bigger than myself. When young people are regarded as integral to the life of a church, the camera lens goes panoramic.

My hope is that this book can contribute in some small way to building momentum, initiated by God Himself who engages in what looks from our limited perspective risky behaviour, forsaking the tried and tested in calling young lives to step forward. As they step forward, fearless in many respects, not carrying the disappointments and insecurities age seems to clock up, I want to do the best I can as the supporting cast.

Which leads me to curling.

Not the morning hair styling routine, but the Winter Olympic sport. 2014 was a great year to watch the event, primarily because Great Britain stayed in it for the long haul, with the men's team winning silver, and the women securing bronze. Sadly, my 2018 Winter Olympics came to an abrupt close when we lost in the semi-finals. For those who missed

Preface

it, curling entails a player sliding a polished, granite stone (like a giant hockey puck with a handle) down a 45m long strip of ice towards a target of concentric circles. It is similar in many respects to bowls; however, a key difference is that once the stone is launched, the team can influence its progression by sending *sweepers* ahead of the stone. Their motion is pretty comical, scrubbing the ice with brooms to change its physical state. As I was watching on my iPad, it dawned on me.

I play a much smaller role than I like to think that I do.

Me? No. I'm not the main event, but I am part of the team. I get to run ahead and do what I can, to influence trajectories and remove obstacles. I love how John the Baptist recognised this in himself, not as the promised one, nor the prophet, but simply as "the voice of one calling in the desert, 'Make straight the way of the Lord'" (John 1:23). That's my job. And it's yours too. Grab a broom from the closet and sweep what we can out of the way, so that God's work through young people and the church can go unhindered. I am limited by time, energy, priorities, and my own imagination of what could be—none of which bother God, who, in the old language of the Authorized Version of Ephesians 3:20, is "able to do *exceeding abundantly* above all that we ask or think." The double compound found in the Greek is not emphasised in some more modern translations, but it is important. Exceedingly vital in importance. Have I made my point?

Whatever you think God can do, He can do more.

God surpasses our own vision and creativity, and that's impressive when you have a hyperactive imagination like me.

I have written what I hope is a fun book to read, packed with story after story from my own experiences as I wrestle with wider theory and the depths of the biblical witness. I hope that my thoughts will benefit Christian youth work through the church, whether you are an employer, employee, volunteer, or have-a-go hero. Having stood on both sides of the pastor—youth worker divide, I also try to connect with the heart behind both that often gets misconstrued by the other. Finally, it is written in light of persistent and comprehensive sociological and philosophical change in our Western cultures. Rather than fear for the future, faith should be our response. God, our Father, does not change, yet He has written change into our DNA as Christians. When Martin Luther nailed his 95 theses to the church door in Wittenberg back in 1517 to challenge the sale of indulgences, he would have known the importance of starting well. The first read:

Preface

"When our Lord and Master Jesus Christ said "Repent," he intended that the entire life of believers should be repentance."

Transformation, at the heart of a biblical understanding of repentance, is something we are all about as Christians. Like Luther, let's encourage the roll out in our corporate lives, too. Many of us sitting in the metaphorical, virtual, or literal pews dream about what church could be like, and my vision has always been to see the notion of every member ministry, or body ministry, realised. The good stuff about church often gets lost in worship wars and members meetings, and our media and politicians seem to have a lot of hate for it. Maybe because the media rarely sees the church stripped back. Rather, social media, politicians and news outlets throw the spotlight on cassocked men defrocked for historical sex offenses, gleaming-dentured preachers promising great wealth if you would but sow a small seed into their ministries, the Florida pastor threatening to burn copies of the Koran, and placards directing people to hell at the funerals of soldiers. This happens. The minority get the majority of air-time. But if we can expose the church for what it really is, a better narrative will emerge. Maybe one day Jesus' words will be fully realised, that as we demonstrate love for one another (for who despises their own body? Ephesians 5:29), all people will know that we are His disciples" (John 13:35).

Language can be problematic when talking about the church, as typically we have the one generic word that is used by all to mean very different things. We might consider church being on a continuum, with a definitive sociological understanding at one end, what Dulles refers to as the institutional model of church, and a transcendent understanding at the other, what Dulles refers to as the church as mystical communion.[1] The sociologist observes things such as attendance, denominations and rituals, focusing on the horizontal relationships between people, and how they organize themselves and interact with buildings. The mystic emphasizes and conceptualizes the experience, focussing in particular on the vertical relationship between humanity and God where relational ties are not institutional but pneumatological—the work of the Holy Spirit (Ephesians 4:3).

One tension is that Jesus rarely spoke of the church. His first recorded use of what we translate *church* is in Matthew 16:18, saying to his disciple, "you are Peter (Greek: *Petros*), and on this rock (Greek: *Petra*) I will build my church." First, we should note that it is written in the singular. Jesus is speaking of a universal image of church, that belongs to himself, reflected

---

1. See Dulles, *Models of the Church*, chapters 2 and 3.

Preface

in the 381 AD Niceno-Constantinopolitan Creed: "We believe in one, holy, catholic and apostolic Church." These "Four Marks of the Church" act as a benchmark for us; one in Christ; holy, or set apart "because it has been called out (*ekklesia*) by Christ himself and continues to be called out"[2]; universal in the sense that we "orient ourselves so that we consider and participate in the entire church—past, present and future, east, west north and south—and to recognize our presence there"[3]; and apostolic in the sense of established through the teaching of the apostles and continuing to be sent into the world. Secondly, the word play on Peter's name is obvious in the Greek text but lost on the modern reader. The question is whether *this rock* refers to Peter himself, or his confession in verse 16 that "You are the Christ, the Son of the living God" that Jesus emphatically blesses Peter for[4]—a spiritual truth spiritually discerned (1 Corinthians 2:13-15). This satisfies me more than the previous explanation. The universal church is seen through Paul's writings when he, for example, reminds husbands to love their wives "just as Christ loved the church" (Ephesians 5:25), and confesses that he does not deserve to be called an apostle "because I persecuted the church of God" (1 Corinthians 15:9).

The only other use of "church" by Jesus in the gospels is in Matthew 18:17 in the context of unrepentant disciples, that "if they refuse to listen, tell it to the church . . ." Here we have the local expression of the universal, reflected in Paul's description of "the church that meets at their house" in Romans 16:5, and when "he landed at Caesarea, he went up and greeted the church, and then went down to Antioch" (Acts 18:22). This local expression is by far the more frequent use of the word for church.

Add to this complexity the issue that our word "church" is not actually an accurate translation of the Greek *ekklesia* and we find ourselves wrestling through the muddy waters of church history. This word has both a secular and Jewish background[5] and is constructed from *ek* (out of) and *kaleo* (calling), which from about the 5th Century BC referenced the city assembly. In fact, the 1526 AD Tyndale bible used "congregation," or "assembly," to translate *ekklesia*, which appears over a hundred times in the New Testament. The actual Greek word behind "church" is *kuriakos*, meaning "house

---

2. Humphrey, "One, Holy, Catholic and Apostolic," 142.

3. Humphrey, "One, Holy, Catholic and Apostolic," 145.

4. For a detailed consideration of the text see Nolland, *The Gospel of Matthew*, loc. 16:18.

5. Erickson, *Christian Theology*, 1031.

of the Lord" or "belonging to the Lord"—which isn't used in the New Testament until the 16th Century. Is it any wonder that people have to remind themselves that the church is the people, not the building!

Much has gotten lost in translation.

For these reasons, the use of metaphor becomes all the more salient, and it is the notion of the body of Christ which arrests the attention of this book. It's worth noting that even here the language is not straightforward, as it can,

> "refer to the sacrificial death of Christ on the cross [Romans 7:4]; sometimes it describes the fellowship experienced in the Lord's Supper [1 Corinthians 10:16]; and more often it refers to the body of believers whose unity was made possible through that cross and is beautifully expressed in that fellowship meal."[6]

It is clear, then, that the metaphor "is not a single expression with an unchanging meaning. Paul's thought remains extremely flexible and elastic,"[7] and so I offer an exploration of the third of those definitions in Paul's theology, notably from Ephesians 4 and 1 Corinthians 9 and 12, yet never lose sight of the tensions and challenges that exist in youth work practice, pointing towards a way of conceptualising ministry that really works. In 2015 Fernando Arzola contended that "Protestant youth ministry has all but erased ecclesiology from its theological radar."[8] *Looking Good Naked: Youth Work and the Body of Christ* picks up the radar and locks on to the signal, aiming to encourage and inspire Christians about working with young people, rooting it not in a particular youth work model or methodology, but in the concept of the church as the body of Christ. This is not youth work plus, but full-*bodied* expression of the work of Christ. At the end of most chapters, I pose a few questions for reflection and discussion, and also list some action points—things that you can put into practice where you are. This reflects the overall dynamic of the book.

Amongst the myriad of presents that Ben (one of our ever-present types in youth ministry) received on his welcome to the teens was a soft-play mini-soccer-ball. Soft-play is a misnomer. Gathering a dozen teenagers in a cramped hall for a game with a soft-play ball equates to battle-field carnage. The funny thing was, Ben wouldn't let anyone play with it. In fact, it sat for months in the same place next to the fireplace. He explained to me,

6. Watson, *I Believe in the Church*, 96.
7. Minear, *Images of the Church*, 173.
8. Arzola, "Ecclesial View," 113.

Preface

"If we play with it, it will get ruined."

"You're right," I agree. "That's what happens when you put your foot through a ball in the yard. But isn't that the point of having a soccer ball?"

What is the end goal of Christian theology? Just a bunch of religious formulas and tight doctrines to burden life? No. Good theology grows our relationship with Jesus and his body, ending in *doxology*—an expression of praise to God—which according to Romans 12 is about how we live and love. Theology must find its feet in action. The following pages are just spilt ink unless they stimulate better and more informed practice. "God spoke… the world began!" (Psalm 33:9 NLT).

Ironically, I have an unused, unscuffed, full size soccer ball sitting at home. It's aging well, tattooed with the names of every young person from a small group as a leaving gift, including Ben. Sadly, my analogies are only so good, but those captured in the Bible inspire me continually. I hope that the metaphor of the body of Christ breathes a new confidence for you as you play your small part on the team, in making this world a better place in preparation for the next.

—**Andy du Feu, 2019**

Acknowledgements

LOOKING GOOD NAKED WOULD not be possible without the contributions of so many:

the hundreds of young people who I have had the privilege of knowing over the course of nearly 25 years in youth work and ministry, who have challenged my assumptions and biases, many of whom are now simply friends;

the many partners in youth work and ministry, who have compensated for my weaknesses, pushed me to use my own abilities, prayed for me and challenged me, and been there in the highs and lows;

the parents, churches and organisations that have believed in me and trusted me with their young people;

conversation partners, whether long since having walked this planet (C.S. Lewis, King David, Oswald Chambers, etc.), or very much still in the pink;

my colleagues at Moorlands College and further afield who are a source of encouragement, constantly helping me raise my game, and many of whom have taken time to read drafts;

my family, who help me be a better man;

my Lord and Savior, Jesus Christ, the "appointed head over everything for the church, which is his body, the fullness of him who fills everything in every way" (Ephesians 1:22-23).

1

Don't forget to floss
Why we need a robust ecclesiology

THE BAD NEWS

WOULD YOU PREFER TO start with good news or bad? I default to the latter, based on a simple rationale that it may not be *that* bad as news goes, and I would rather finish on a high. So, the bad news for Christian youth workers, church leaders, denominations and Christian youth agencies, complete with an apology:

There is no specific "theology of youth work", nor a compelling "Biblical model for youth ministry" that easily emerges from the pages of inspired Scripture.

I'm sorry.

The lack of clear theological basis is bad news, because our place at the ecclesiological table is flimsy at best. Without that protection, we tend to dress to impress, to cover up our embarrassed nakedness and nagging insecurities in front of church boards, elders, parents and even each other with clever theological models, cutting-edge tech, and inflated stats. Consider how many church-based youth work roles are tied to a 1 to 3 year contract, whereas the church leader will typically be on a continuous contract. According to Ron Belsterling, youth pastors are rarely seen as *real* pastors, and the role is regarded as a stepping stone.[1] He goes on to point to how church leaderships can undervalue the position, noting that "most church leaders

---

1. Belsterling, *A Defense of Youth Ministry*, 51-3.

wouldn't dream of using a doctor with in-house training. How can elders be fine with such an approach for their youth ministry leaders[?]"[2] Think also how youth ministry is undermined by its own self-conscious "experts", regarded by one as today's "horse drawn buggy."[3] Talk about body-shaming your peers.

Flimsy is generous. If only Paul had included youth workers in his list of offices in Ephesians 4: apostles, prophets, evangelists, pastors, teachers, . . . and *youth workers?* Maybe not. Or had the great reformers re-discovered Paul's youth work skills with Eutychus or Timothy, perhaps we would have a chance. But without a defined, consistent and ubiquitous role, our position is downright precarious. I am not surprised.

Why?

Primarily because adolescence as we understand it is a social construct of late-modernity, which "begins in biology and ends in culture,"[4] and I am cautious in my use of the term, as it can easily lead to young people being "objectified, categorized and judged."[5] Wayne Rice goes further, calling it an "artificial category" that leads to "stereotyping and infantilising teenagers."[6] Simply put, we created it. Mark Smith suggests that it was "the technical demands of the economy [that] produced the need for ever longer periods of training and apprenticeship," and "it was not until the late nineteenth century that 'adolescence' came into anything like widespread useage."[7] Transitions into work or family responsibilities have slipped to as late as 35 years old if we are to believe Jefferey Arnett's work[8], with some suggesting that, "the extension of adolescence has expanded so boundlessly that many teens no longer have any realistic sense of what they're ultimately preparing for, or that they are preparing for something."[9]

However, this does generalize Western culture rather than capture a universal truth—a 14 year old carer would profoundly disagree with Arnett for starters. Roll the clock back to first century Palestine, or the period

---

2. Belsterling, *A Defense of Youth Ministry*, 5.
3. Ostreicher, *Youth Ministry 3.0*, 25.
4. Santrock, *Adolescence*, 28-9.
5. Wyn and White, *Rethinking Youth*, 57.
6. Rice, *Reinventing Youth Ministry*, 43.
7. Smith, *Developing Youth Work*, 1.
8. See Jefferey Arnett's notion of a new stage of life, namely emerging adulthood (aka extended adolescence) in Arnett, *Emerging Adulthood*.
9. Allen and Allen, *Escaping the Endless Adolescence*, x.

of the Old Testament Patriarchs, and the idea of compulsory schooling, disposable income and trading cards would find no purchase. Moses had to deal with whinging adults, not rowdy teens, because they didn't exist in the way we think of them today. That's not to say that a child would turn 11 years old and a year later hit 18, skipping years of puberty. It's not hard to imagine, for example, that the 14-year-old Jesus had an outbreak of spots (self-healing is not evident in the Gospel accounts of the Messiah, and certainly not before He turned 30). The transition from child to adult has always taken place whether spiritually, physically, intellectually, emotionally or socially; it is simply that the concept of adolescence is comparatively recent, and not experienced universally. For most young people, the freedom of childhood was exchanged for the duties of adulthood as soon as they were capable of work, and this holds true in a number of countries, particularly where educational provision is poor. In the West, dominant social forces led to the introduction of child labor laws and mandatory schooling, which have continued to extend in the 21st century, lengthening this period of formation, leading some to contend that, "adolescents today inhabit a world largely unknown to adults."[10] Research since the 90s has pointed towards the notion of extended adolescence, with the characteristic elements of the teen pushing into the twenties and early thirties. Borgman comments that "We are forcing children and adolescents to live in the limbo of pseudo-adulthood; true adulthood is more elusive than ever before."[11] While a young person may legally be regarded an adult at 18, maturity might be little more than just physical.

Kidulthood[12] has become a lived reality in the West.

Figure 1 is wrong in every way. When I was working in urban youth and children's ministry in New Jersey at 18, people would say, "Andy, you've got an old head on young shoulders." While, sadly, no one says that anymore, it was a massive encouragement to my younger self. The opposite would be offensive, unless you are called Caleb whose youthful vigor at a mere 85 is noted in Joshua 14:6-13. We will return to this idea later, but to summarize, a child's head on an older body might access the adult world, but not have the emotional and intellectual maturity to contribute meaningfully.

---

10. Hersch, *A Tribe Apart*, viii.

11. Borgman, *When Kumbaya is Not Enough*, 72.

12. The term was popularized by the eponymous 2006 film documenting the lives of a group of West London teenagers.

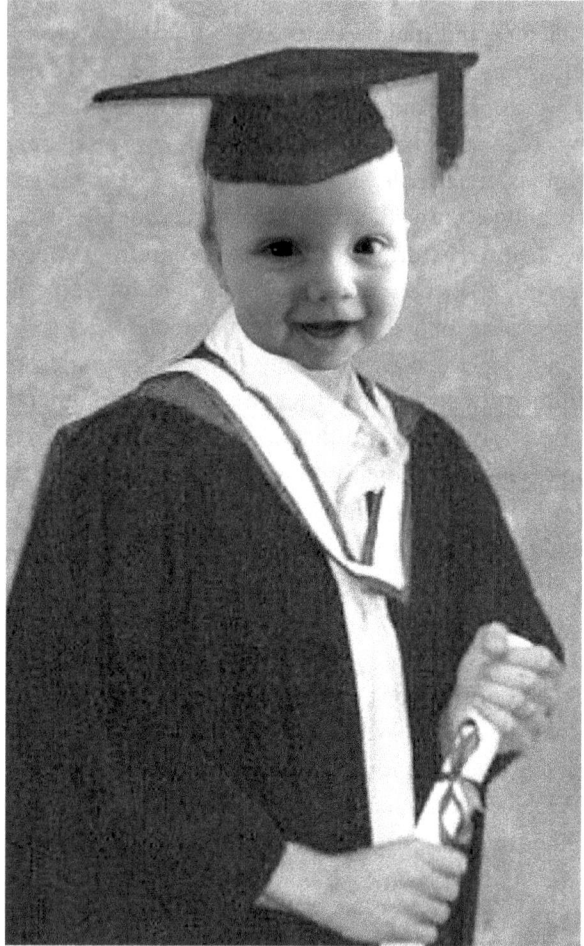

Figure 1: Young Head on Old Shoulders

Nowhere does the Bible record legal age in a clear manner, although a brief exploration of terminology from the Old Testament provides us with some clues. In its short reflection, Ecclesiastes 11:9 packs in three different Hebrew words for youth:

"Rejoice, O young man, in your youth, and let your heart cheer you in the days of your youth." (ESV)

Young man (Hebrew: *bachuwr*) indicates they are of fighting age and allowed to fight in the army, which means 20 years old (e.g. Numbers 1:22). This is also the age where the sanctuary contribution came into effect (Exodus 30:12-14). Before that threshold, boys were considered "grown up" upon the first signs of beard growth on the cheeks, and women considered mature on the appearance of breasts. The first use of the word *youth* (Hebrew: *yalduwth*) is actually translated *childhood* in the NASB and refers to a definite time frame, while the second *youth* (Hebrew: *bechurowth*) points to young people as a collective, or in the more abstract sense. The Old Testament has different words for children, and these distinctions are further highlighted by the ceremonial value of men and women as broken down by age in Leviticus 27:1-8:

Age	Male	Female
60+yrs	15 Shekels	10 Shekels
20-60yrs	50 Shekels	30 Shekels
5-20yrs	20 Shekels	10 Shekels
1m-5yrs	5 Shekels	3 Shekels

Figure 2: Ceremonial Value by Age and Gender in Shekels of Silver (Leviticus 27:1-8)

Outraged?

Remember, first, that you are looking at this through the lens of the 21st Century. Second, the values were set according to the capacity for work of the individual, what we can loosely refer to as potential productivity, and some of these are disturbingly reflected by our own culture, if we just take time to look beneath the surface. Think for a moment how society increasingly regards the elderly as a burden, how the rights of the unborn and the "best interests of the child" are often ignored, and how the gender pay gap still exists. Consider also how adolescence, not too dissimilar to the 5-20 years category from Leviticus, is one filled with tension. On the one hand, this period is characterized by disposable income and parental influence that marketers aggressively exploit, being the exclusive focus of a fashion and cosmetic industry worth billions, and by freedom and energy that the media machine uses ... and abuses.

Esther had grown up in our youth work programmes and had a great set of vocal chords. Well above average, she made mum and dad proud at the school show. Feeling the pull of the stage, she desperately wanted to sign up for X-Factor. The problem was, she possessed a great singing voice, just not a top-1% singing voice, and her image was certainly not Susan Boyle, neither was it close to Little Mix or Kelly Clarkson. She would be chewed up and spat out as soon as her ratings dropped. Thankfully, she listened to the pleas of her parents and the yammering of her youth workers and focused on other pursuits.

Yet on the other hand, absurdly paradoxical age restrictions abound (Appendix 1 lists many of these), youth are literally left to their own devices but are heavily surveilled by transnational companies and law-enforcement agencies, and the prospect of long term career paths is increasingly bleak.[13] It is tough being a teenager in today's world—an illusion of importance and responsibility, yet you cannot buy a hacksaw IRL for your school design project.[14] Go figure.

There has always been tension between young and old, with Socrates conceding around 400 BC that "if the whole world depends on today's youth, I can't see the world lasting another 100 years" and Peter the Hermit in 1114 AD complaining that "Youth has no regard for old age and the wisdom of the centuries is looked down upon both as stupid and foolishness." However, it is evident that the twentieth century experienced a rapid escalation of that tension, with social structures adapting to the emergence of the teen (a term coined in the 1940's to describe a new generation with money in their pockets and more leisure time than ever before), and the church has been no exception. Charles Kraft coined the term "generation gap" in the late 1960s to capture a growing problem for the evangelical church in reaching and keeping young people,[15] by which time organisations such as YMCA (1844), Scripture Union (1867), Crusaders (1906), Young Life (1941), and Youth for Christ (1946) were already very much active working with young people. It is worth noting that, unlike the "Jesus movement" (circa 1967), "these had existed as 'auxiliaries' to the mainstream church, and had not attempted to establish fresh models of being church in their own right."[16] Before Robert Raikes and Hannah More, regarded as early proponents of the Sunday School circa 1790,[17] the notion

---

13. The rate of unemployment in the UK has fallen from a 2011 high of 21.9%, with 1 million people aged 16 to 24 unemployed, the highest figure in 23 years, to 11.9% in 2017. See 'UK unemployment increases to 2.62m' *BBC News*, 16 November 2011, http://www.bbc.co.uk/news/business-15747103 and Andrew Powell, 'Youth Unemployment Statistics', *House of Commons Library: Briefing Paper*, Number 5871, 21 March 2018.

14. True story! From my own experience as a pastor and youth worker at 25 years old. The well-known retailer demanded proof I was over 18—I gave them my wedding finger . . .

15. See Kraft, *Christianity in Culture*, 378-9.

16. Hilborn and Bird, *God and the Generations*, 5.

17. See the excellent material on *infed*, maintained by the George Williams College

of age-segregation in church barely existed, let alone a church for young people. Children would sit quietly with their parents at services that had no puppets, action songs or prayer stations. Without even having to rattle my hippocampus I can think of 40 young people that I have worked with who would explode in such an environment. I can think of some adults who would raise hell, too. Sue, a parent of three under 11s, came to me and said that unless the youth work improved, they would be moving churches. It was a consumeristic punch to the idealist stomach. As a pastor I was all too aware that people choose a church not based on the teaching, fellowship, location or commitment to world mission, but on the quality of child and youth work provision, with worship styles claiming the runner-up prize, and this often done before they ever step foot in the door.

In the US, and in more recent years, in the UK, we have sought to find biblically congruent models of youth work and the church, and defended our choices, yet we often end up with either the pragmatic or the ad hoc. Simply put, we go for what seems to work, pouring our money and energy into the areas that seem to satisfy the stakeholders, or we put it together on the fly, working reactively rather than proactively. Few churches go beyond the vision statement to having a strategic plan to see that vision come to life, and even fewer youth ministries understand their real purpose theologically and philosophically, and how they are going to actualize it.

THE GOOD NEWS

Feeling slightly ambivalent about the bad, let's consider the good news: youth ministry piggybacks on tried and tested theological concepts and rides the waves of missiology and Christology. Others have done the hard work, and when youth work shows up late in the ecclesiological day, the tools are already laid out for us. Granted, we need to sharpen them and make some tweaks here and there, but we are good to go and for many of us, we just get on with the task before us. For example, so much has been written and explored around the concept of incarnational ministry that you might think this was the sole property of youth ministry[18] but the approach is seen back in the 19th Century when missionary, Hudson Taylor, decided to adopt the native Chinese clothes and pigtail with shaven forehead. This

http://infed.org/mobi/hannah-more-sunday-schools-education-and-youth-work/.

18. See Root, *Revisiting Relational Youth Ministry*, and Griffiths, *Models for Youth Ministry* for two very different takes on incarnational ministry.

gave him an audience without the fuss of a typical western-style missionary of the day, although he was known as *the black devil* due to his trench coat! Incarnational ministry is regarded as both Christological (rooted in the person, words and actions of Christ) and missiological (based on the mandate to take the gospel to the world). We have simply found a home for it within youth ministry under the banner of relational work, which is one of the primary approaches in youth work practice.

The art of conversation and relationship building is one that means that you can get better at youth work even as you get older and move further and further away from being somewhat similar to a peer—helpful at 18 or 19. You listened to the same music, watched the same shows, and laughed at the same comedians. I learned my lesson using what I thought was a hilarious sketch from Harry Enfield.

Young person: "Who?"
Me: "Harry Enfield. You know (switch voice to falsetto) *Tree! Tree!*"
Young people stare at me rather blankly.
#Awks.

A very small number of you are smiling right now. But most of you saw tumbleweed pass in front of your eyes. A quick IMDB[19] search will tell you that *Harry Enfield and Chums* lit up British playground conversations in the 1990s but is limited to nostalgic British (Grand?) Father's Day sales nowadays. Relational work and conversation locate ministry in the life and times of the young person, and as much as it might seem to come naturally to some, it needs continual work to stay fresh. That's one reason why I keep doing youth work. How can I train people in youth and community work if I'm not involved at the coalface?

FINDING YOUR FEET IN A CROSS-CURRENT

For those who might be wondering about my surname, I am not French. My name originates from Jersey, the largest of the Channel Islands, where *du Feu* is relatively common. A slight aside is that, with Andy deriving from the Greek for *Man*, my name literally means, *Man of the Fire*. Cool. Thanks, Mum and Dad. One of my favorite locations in Jersey is *la Corbière*. It's a lighthouse that you can walk to when the tide is out and the path is uncovered (see Figure 3), but on no account should you ignore the warning that

---

19. The ubiquitous Internet Movie Database—the go-to resource for TV and film stars, directors, etc.

sounds when the tide has turned. Should you get caught at the lighthouse when the tide turns, my advice is simple: Move. Now. Even with a few inches of water creeping over the path, the danger is real. The area is known for its powerful cross-tide, with waves fierce and unpredictable, yet there is a rugged beauty to the place that brings people back time after time.

Figure 3: La Corbière

Likewise, if you have done youth work for any length of time, you will have experienced those sessions where you wonder what the point is. One Wednesday night sticks out in my mind for the volatile atmosphere that sat like a low-lying cloud. When the first fight erupted, I fool-hardily stepped right in between the two angry teenagers, and simultaneously got punched in the face and lower back. They weren't aiming at me. Equipment got damaged, a window smashed, and most of the volunteers were verbally abused. Time to quit. It's not worth it. Time to throw in the towel. Restless night follows restless night. Yet somehow next Wednesday you are back in the mix. It's a love-hate relationship.

- When Ryan opened up about his manipulative but absent dad.
- Tina who hated me from day one, staying in touch well into her twenties.

- Hearing that Matthew is now leading the CU at his University.
- Amie's decision to risk social exclusion not to take part in sexting at a prestigious school.
- The many failures on my part that God provided grace for.

These make the pain worthwhile. However, 2 Corinthians 4:17 inspires us to persevere, to go the extra mile, "for our light and momentary troubles are achieving for us an eternal glory that far outweighs them all. 18 So we fix our eyes not on what is seen . . . "

The writer of the book of Hebrews expresses how we can derive motivation and passion, not from the ministry highs, but the pain of the valley and the promise of what will be, echoing Jesus, "who for the joy set before him endured the cross" (Hebrews 12:2). There is a possibility that these words formed part of an early Christian creed[20] and no wonder, given the way that Jesus foretold his own suffering, modelling the resilience needed to follow him.

Youth work and ministry is growing up, but there are some significant challenges that threaten to take its feet from under it. Since the late 1980s churches have been persuaded at a deep level that after the pastor / vicar / minister, the most critical role is that of someone to work with the young people. In the US the youth pastor or leader is an assumed part of most staff teams of bigger churches. In the lower half of the UK, this typically means a full or part time youth role. In the north this is more likely to be invested adults in a voluntary capacity—that army of ordinary superheroes. Granted, despite youth roles being increasingly blended with family / community / young adults / children, the motivation is to ensure the church has a future. Augment that with the reality that most significant faith decisions are made before the 18th birthday[21] and it's clear that youth work is still high on the list of ecclesial priorities.

At the time when churches began to realize the need for youth investment in the mid to late 20th Century, youth work emerged as an academic discipline in its own right, and professionalization in the UK was a step in the right direction to ensure safe and robust practice complete with terms and conditions for workers. A purpose statement for youth work was established and refined, recognising the youth worker's role to:

---

20. Ellingworth, *The Epistle to the Hebrews*, 641.

21. Brewster and McDonald, *Children—The Great Omission*, suggest that while this is true, less than 15% of our efforts are directed to ministry amongst children.

"Enable young people to develop holistically, working with them to facilitate their personal, social and educational development, to enable them to develop their voice, influence and place in society and to reach their full potential."[22]

Back in 1991, the *2nd Ministerial Conference for the Youth Service* outlined four core values that underpin this mission statement:

1. Voluntary Participation,
2. Empowerment,
3. Informal Education,
4. Equality of Opportunity.

I made the point in 2018 that, "Youth ministry literature, particularly from the US, makes little or no attempt to engage with professional approaches to youth work [whereas] Christian youth work [primarily in the UK] has a relationship with youth work theory, histories and professionalism, however explicit or not that is."[23]

Recognising a gulf between so-called *secular* youth work[24] and youth ministry, Danny Brierley attempted to "baptize" the core values in his 2003 book, Joined Up. He demonstrated how each value could be argued from a biblical position, contending that, "the life and work of Christ Jesus makes them biblically justified,"[25] before adding a fifth: *Incarnational Ministry*. Baptising the secular is a deeply theological practice, exercised, no less, than by the writers of the Bible. Consider Paul quoting Greek poets in Acts 17. He acknowledges the overlapping truth, recognising that, "as your own poets have said, 'We are his offspring.'" It's the start of the 5th line, verbatim, of an astronomical poem of Aratus, circa 300BC. It would have been expressed in a pantheistic sense, but Paul redeems the truth within to point to the one true and living God. We now use these "baptized" lyrics in our churches about God, in whom "we live, move and have our being" (verse 28) as if Paul authored them!

The problem was two-fold:

---

22. National Youth Agency, *Professional Validation: Guidance and Requirements*, 2019, 1.5.

23. du Feu, "Making room at the table."

24. I would argue that the word, *secular*, is not that helpful at all, because it creates an *us and them* perspective.

25. Brierley, *Joined Up*, 135.

First, as we have seen, incarnational ministry is just one theological model. Why not have Trinitarian / Christological / kenotic / creational youth ministry instead? A rationale for relational approaches can pretty much be built through any of these, so how is incarnational the Christian distinctive, especially when Hinduism also has an incarnational framework? Yes, God was made flesh in Jesus Christ, "being made in human likeness [and] found in appearance as a man" (Philippians 2:7-8), but the Supreme Being, Vishnu, manifests in human form, in order to bring peace and protection when the world is lost in chaos and destruction.

Secondly, the core values of youth work were established on the shifting sands of social policy and are open to theological critique. "Always contested territory, youth work's meaning and methodology became increasingly blurred to the point where, within the structures state policymakers were willing to fund or at least endorse, its distinctive features were masked, denied, dismissed as no longer relevant - or changed radically."[26] After massive cuts to the Youth Service decimated front line services in the UK under the coalition government and put some youth work courses in jeopardy, Michael Gove announced in July 2013 the dissolution of the seemingly rock-solid marriage between youth work and the Department for Education, and arranged a marriage with the Cabinet Office[27] meaning that youth work was more in line with the latest government social policy rather than being steered primarily by those invested in education. With second marriages typically less reliable, it was no surprise that youth work moved again just three years later, this time to the Department for Culture, Media and Sports. Youth work in the UK has an identity crisis. Indeed, British youth work authority, Smith, asserted that the term, "youth work" was born with the [government-funded] "youth service" and has died with the "youth service".[28] The statistics are bleak, as Bernard Davies comments:

> "Some of the most telling evidence of the Youth Service cuts came from the trade union Unison in two reports published in July 2014 and August 2016. The first revealed that by then nationally at least 350 youth centres had closed, 41,000 youth service places and 35,000 hours of outreach work had been lost, and more than 2000 youth worker jobs had been abolished. Two years later, drawing on

---

26. Davies, *Austerity, Youth Policy*, 14.

27. Press release, 3rd July 2013, Gov.uk, https://www.gov.uk/government/news/cabinet-office-to-take-on-responsibility-for-cross-government-youth-policy

28. Smith, "Is there a Future".

returns from 180 of the 210 relevant authorities, updated figures revelled that over 600 youth centres had closed, nearly 139,000 places for young people had been lost, and 3652 youth worker jobs abolished."[29]

As I write, very few Local Authorities still provide youth services, and these are declining rapidly, although there is a hope that we are reaching a low-tide mark, with efforts to secure a base-level requirement for youth work currently being recommended by an All-Party Parliamentary Group inquiry into the role and function of youth work.[30]

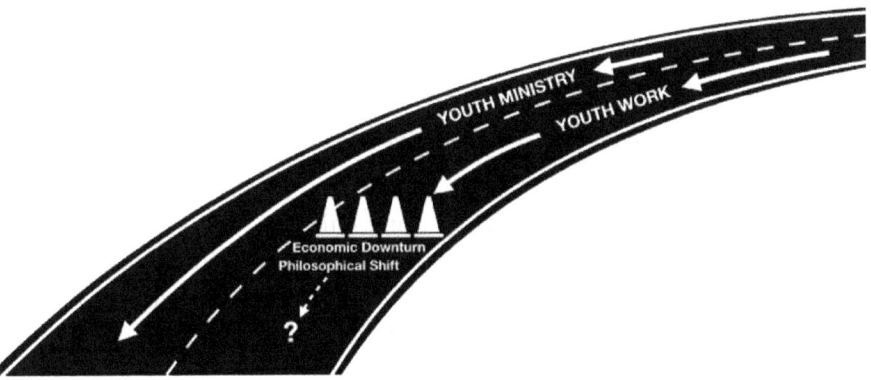

Figure 4: Cross Tides in Youth Work

These cross tides sweeping over the youth work road have caught out many who didn't hear the double-barrelled warning in both the philosophical shift as well as the economic downturn. The church must realize that while these currents have decimated the Youth Service, they do not show partiality. While Bright and Bailey are right in asserting that, "the relative political independence that Christian youth work enjoys continues to harbour many of youth work's core values from the policy initiatives that have attempted to erode the profession's traditional practices, which are founded on relational principles that seek to promote learning, democracy, justice and action,"[31] funding for UK Christian youth projects has been hit. There

---

29. Davies, *Austerity, Youth Policy*, 73.

30. All-Party Parliamentary Group on Youth Affairs, *Youth Work Inquiry: Final Report*, April 2019, 8.

31. Bright and Bailey, "Youth Work and the Church", 145.

may also be some impact on church-based work as givers tighten their financial belts.

CALLING ALL UNDERDOGS

The youth work landscape sketched out above is uncomfortable reading, and far more has been detailed about the decline of youth ministry in the US, with the issue ultimately located in insecurities about our identity. Davies could speak for the church-based scene when he writes that the

> "underdog status stemmed from a wider and long-standing political and indeed cultural perception of 'youth'. This focussed overwhelmingly on their 'transitions' - on their need (and indeed obligation) to become productive workers, responsible parents and law-abiding and 'contributing' citizens. The result was a policy-making view of the young as merely citizens in the making with reduced rights."[32]

The problem with the underdog status is that we begin to see ourselves in that way, embracing the label, fighting for the scraps from the table. Jesus commends the Syrophoenician woman for such a disposition, but we are not awkward dinner guests turning up late without an invite. We have a seat at the table, welcomed by the Father of the house, and missed when we fail to turn up.

My contention in this book is that, rather than find a fresh model for youth ministry, yet another set of clothes to put on, we need to return with renewed vision to something as secure as a lighthouse against the storms and rising tides and look at youth work's relationship with the church. Chap Clark agrees, contending that "we are being forced by society and by real people to go deeper and to find more stable theological footing for not only what and how we do our work but also why we do it and where it fits into God's plan."[33] I believe that the local church as the body of Christ is the hope of the world because its basis is embedded in Scripture rather than social policy. Smith contends powerfully that, "state funding for youth and community work is over. Its future is in religious and social movements."[34] As Christians we need to first find our feet, and only then we can handle the

---

32. Davies, *Austerity, Youth Policy*, 6.
33. Clark, *Youth Ministry*, xii.
34. Smith, "Is there a Future".

cross-currents. No wonder Paul writes that our job is to simply stand firm (Ephesians 6:13,14 NIV), or as the Good News Version puts it, "hold your ground." Let's rediscover our footing.

Have the crosscurrents caught God out? In a word: No. God permits authority to nations (Romans 13:1) and "determined beforehand when they should rise and fall, and he determined their boundaries" (Acts 17:26 NLT). Any sense of nationalistic power is limited, as God keeps them on a short leash, with Job commenting that God "makes the nations great, then destroys them; He enlarges the nations then leads them away" (Job 12:23), laughing at their pretence, "holding them in derision" (Psalm 2:4, ESV), "scoffing at them" (Psalm 2:4, NIV).

As Christians we have often been considered dangerous because, while we pray for those in authority (1 Timothy 2:2) and voluntarily submit to them (Romans 13:5) we recognize that they will not endure, having a primary citizenship (Philippians 3:20) that is not geographically bound (John 18:36-37). Policy, philosophy and people will all pass away, but God's word will remain (1 Corinthians 7:31, Matthew 24:35). This confident perspective frames the biblical narratives and understanding something of the big picture enables us to move forward.

"Do I look good in this?"

Being married for 15+ years, I have experienced second hand the dilemma of what to wear, and on special occasions, the morning routine can be like a fashion show.

Me: "You look . . . *incredible*."

"Do I? OK, I'm not sure. I think I'll try the other one on."

Positive words rarely compensate for a lack of confidence. The right clothes can breed a kind of confidence, but I do not want to rely on the methods and techniques that we can wear, or the technologies that we can dress Christian youth work up in.

Freya was the keynote at a denominational youth event, but as she got up to speak, the projector bulb died. I watched her eyes widen in disbelief, and frantic, hushed exchanges with the tech guys. Stepping into the spotlight, she announced that "tonight is going to be a little different." She lasted little more than 13 minutes before sitting down, her top now a deeper shade of red down her back. In 2014 Michael Bay, producer of the blockbuster movie franchise, *Transformers*, failed epically to *"wing it,"* as he boldly declared he would, when the teleprompter ceased to live up to its name. He tried to piece a sentence together, turned on his heel, and walked out.[35] Wow.

I want us to look good naked; confident in who we are, so that any clothes we put on are simply helping create cultural bridges into communities. Don't worry, this has been a metaphorical picture of the church, the body of Christ, rather than about me turning up to youth group in my birthday suit. It's critical that we are comfortable with our own bodies, and Christian youth work is no different.

I cannot shake my theological commitments and recognize their enduring nature. Davies, one of the key voices in shaping youth work in the UK, recognizes that separating out your personal beliefs from what you do in practice "is not a realistic option,"[36] and from a Christian perspective, Thompson reminds us that "a Christian youth worker, even in a secular setting, cannot take their values off at the door like a coat, but must acknowledge them as a core part of their identity and motivation."[37]

It is easy and useful for churches to look to the professionals, and denominations and Christian organisations to focus on youth work skills but being pragmatic doesn't mean being right. A paucity of spirituality can hide behind a professional veneer, yet I believe the most secure location for youth work and ministry is in authentic Christian community, embedded in the notion of church as God's new community. This is what I refer to as our healthy body image, based on New Testament teaching, notably two key passages from the Apostle Paul's letters to the churches: 1 Corinthians 12, and Ephesians 4, with a focus on verses 11 through to 16. The notion of the body of Christ is just one of many images that the New Testament writers give us for the church, with *family of God, building, precious stones,* and the *bride of Christ* notable alternatives. The body metaphor is perhaps the most sustained image, and was the main definition of the church for Karl Barth, considered by some to be the "church father" of the twentieth century.[38] Crosby sums it up so well, that the "absolutely amazing truth is that God has already supplied us with the means to nourish his people, and yet we find ourselves thinking we can do better."[39] Rice nails it when he

---

35. See http://www.mtv.com/news/articles/1719961/michael-bay-teleprompter-malfunction.html for Bay's own comment on the event!

36. Davies, "The Place of Doubt in Youth Work," 130.

37. Thompson, "Being a Christian Youth Worker," 13-4.

38. Healy, "Logic of Karl Barth's Ecclesiology," 256-7.

39. Cosby, *Giving Up Gimmicks,* 64.

surmizes that "what we have today is not really a youth ministry problem. It's a church problem. Truth is—it always has been a church problem."[40]

It's time to dress down and get back to the essentials.

URBAN CHIC

The early chapters explore some of the underlying concerns and issues with looking good naked. We consider the expectations that point us away from each other towards control; both expectations that are placed on youth workers and ones that emerge from the self. Ultimately, the starting place is theological, and God the one who creates and declares His work *"very good."* Chapter 4 critiques the popular idea of starting out from scratch, recognising that what we wear is not random. Chapter 5 reflects on finding warm bodies to do youth work, and critiques the notion of pastor, both positively and negatively.

Confidence is built up through trying on outfits in the early work, but in chapter 6 the book gains real traction. The church needs a healthy body image, and to be comfortable in its own skin. This is mapped against a critique of the core values of youth work in chapters 7 to 10 which give us the confidence to step out, and take to the city streets in chapter 11, not worrying about what others think about our appearance, *knowing* we can get on with doing what we do best. I hope that some of these ideas turn heads, and get people talking in the spaces they occupy.

---

40. Rice, *Reinventing Youth Ministry*, 144.

2

False Expectations
Why we need clarity about people and roles

HEROES NEED NOT APPLY

THERE IS A DEBATE in the world of comics and big-screen movies as to the real identity of Batman. We know him as rich playboy Bruce Wayne and wonder how others do not make the link—square jaw, deep voice—even the eye shadow cannot disguise him. But the question that haunts us is this:
"Is Batman a Superhero?"

He is thoughtlessly thrown in the box with Spiderman, Superman / woman / boy, Captain Marvel, Hulk, Thor, etc. Yet he has no special powers. What he does possess is an über cool gadget belt. Without his Morgan Freeman-bolstered R&D department, he would be reduced to a make-up-wearing neo-ninja with an attitude problem.

Others disagree. Some suggest that his heightened fighting ability, detective nous and determined pursuit of the villain *are* superhuman. An editorial on fan-site Comicbookmovie.com, suggests that he is so by proxy—he is categorized with the others in the Justice League, for example.[1] A blogger on Herodistrict.com suggests that it is the mythology that surrounds them and, "what sets them apart from any other type of literary character is they exist visually as much as they do textually, and because of this visual component they are now deemed super."[2]

---

1. Ecksmanfan, "Editorial: Is Batman a Superhero?"
2. Mckiernan, "The Problem of Batman: Is Batman a Superhero?"

False Expectations

I will leave you to decide which camp to side with, but maybe his self-perception will settle the debate.

The Flash: "So what's your super-power?"

Bruce Wayne: "I'm rich."[3]

But what has this to do with Christian youth work? A cursory glance at a job database or the back pages of *Youth & Children's Work* magazine reveals that there is an explicit expectation that the person who fits the bill will require Bruce's gadget belt at the very least. There are the odd exceptions, such as the church publication in Figure 5,[4] but they are not the norm.

WEAK YOUTH LEADER NEEDED!

▬▬▬▬Parish Church is looking for a man or woman who may not have every gift in the tool kit, but who loves the Scriptures, and would love to teach Jesus prayerfully and joyfully to young people.

Applicants would...
- Have some training and experience in teaching the Bible to young people.
- Encourage the church to love & give young people a different family experience to their (often broken) homes
- Bring the best out of busy volunteer leaders
- Take gospel enthusiasm to local secondary schools
- Play a part in leading ministry to adults in the life of the church.

 ... whilst prayerfully trusting God's strength to be made perfect in their weakness, and being fully supported by our church and its leaders.
A fair salary and accommodation will be provided.

Figure 5: Superheroes Need Not Apply

Job ads look for professionalism over prayer; competence over character; energy over empathy; decisiveness over depth, even when the employer is marked by amateurism, incompetence, lethargy and indecisiveness. We have bought into the culture where all too often the salary precedes the job description, and job hunters rifle through the ads scanning that all-important figure, ruling out anything below a certain threshold. But what does the salary-first approach say? It tells us something of the expectations and priorities present, often at a subconscious level. A big salary before

---

3. Snyder, *Justice League*.
4. Used with permission

any description might mean the church wants to have a captive audience and hopefully woo the best to interview, but it might come with strings attached. Imagine what expectations might exist when the church know that you are being paid more than the pastor of the church because your job came with JNC[5] terms and conditions! The salary-first approach also puts the contract over calling. A friend who operates a national youth ministry says that only those with a clear sense of calling sign up for a job with them, as the worker must raise part of their own salary. Our bottom line must be more than cold hard cash or an all-inclusive package.

"Weak youth worker needed." That's bold. Would you apply? It would be quite an admission. Many churches declare their desire for competence, and why shouldn't they, given the position they are trying to fill? Many churches want someone who will cover nappy changes through to student digs. Another is looking to pioneer some seriously exciting youth work, but the successful applicant will be expected to help at the café for the elderly, too. Some of the following picks up on the dark side of working with and for churches. Buckle up that belt and tuck in your cape. We need to ride out a storm.

MAKING THE IMPLICIT EXPLICIT

Aside from the money issue, a major reason for the role ambiguity and overload is that many churches have not asked enough questions during the planning stages. This means that they do not know what they really want when they are interviewing, and do not have the cash to employ more than one extra person, so roles are lumped together.

Critical questions unearth the deeper motivations and establish a firmer philosophical and practical base for employing. A few such questions might be:

- Why do we want someone working with young people?
- Do we want someone who works face to face with young people, or who works with volunteers to work with young people?
- Do we want a [*pick from* family / youth / student / children] [leader / pastor / minister / worker / intern]? Why?

---

5. Short for Joint Negotiating Committee, the body that set and keep the terms, conditions and pay grades for youth workers in England and Wales.

- Why those terms? How will the title be understood by the church?
- What are the implications of having an employee?
- What do we anticipate that they will bring to the table that we do not currently possess?
- Are other people doing the same thing in our locality?
- What role will they have in relation to wider leadership structures?
- Who will line-manage them?
- Who are the real stakeholders and investors here?

The formal contract of employment is the one you sign, detailing hours, pay, role, entitlements, etc. However, there is also an informal contract between you and the organisation, often covered by a bland statement such as, "and any other duties relevant to the work of the organisation." There is some give and take here, but too much give on either side reveals a lack of definition to the role before advertising. They might verbally say that you are to "work with our teenagers" but when you arrive there is the clear expectation that you will run the children's holiday club. Expectations are difficult to manage, because they are rarely seen in writing.

These are the implicit expectations, known as the psychological contract. These are not communicated to you on the advert or through the interview process. In fact, you normally stumble upon them by breaking an unwritten rule. There was the unspoken expectation in one place that a Sunday morning youth group would continue to use the lounge of our house because it was church property, even though we had moved in. The building served a higher calling than simply as our home! As servant leaders, there was an implicit expectation that this was an appropriate sacrifice of personal space. While there was an upshot in providing a snug environment for young people, it masked the lack of facilities in the church, delayed real development, and meant making cleaning debris off our mocha lounge carpet part and parcel of our Sunday experience.

The psychological contract comes into play when you have done a weekend away with young people and believe that you should have some reward for 72 hours of graft. Reward is open to interpretation and might be monetary (think Christmas or performance bonuses), days of in lieu, public recognition, or some creative way to demonstrate appreciation. When this is not forthcoming (and it is incredibly difficult to ask for post-hoc), it can breed resentment and reduce your sense of commitment. Why should you break your back for this ungrateful lot? A friend of mine worked for a major car manufacturer known for its family-like qualities and atmosphere, evidenced by how it treated many of its workers when the car industry hit hard times during the late noughties. However, he was quick to warn me that this was to some extent illusion. Ultimately, they are a business and the financial bottom line means the lay-off is all the more painful if you believed you were more than just an employee and actually a family member. Few church leaders stop to ask what the bottom line is for their church, and so break ups, divisions and terminated contracts are all the worse when it boils down to money, reputation or tradition.

In a different youth ministry, it quickly became apparent that anything we bought was up for grabs for other groups, because our budget was actually an illusion created by the treasurer, and not part of the church budget. Our new console took a beating from an unsupervized rabble, and I pulled it out of the cupboard more than once to find the batteries were flat and the power-cable damaged. Not possessing extra-sensory perception (mind-reading in common parlance), misunderstanding unspoken rules that were not part of the induction process, and missing functions that you did not realize you had to be at all point towards your mortality. But superheroes are on the shopping list of almost every church and Christian charity. This works directly against the body imagery, which possesses a distinct anatomy, and clarity over how each part relates to each other. Note that in 1 Corinthians 12:21 Paul didn't say, "The hand-eye-mouth cannot say to the nose-knee-intestine, 'I don't need you!'" We need the many parts that add up to one body.

OUTSIDE IS THE NEW INSIDE

One of the biggest tensions that I have seen is over *who* the target group are, *how* objectives will be achieved, and *what* the implications are.

Over a coffee Matty told me how four weeks prior they had an influx of 40 young people who had no connection with the well-oiled, very middle-class church. The local youth center had closed, and they had decided *en masse* to try out the Friday night club. The first night was intense, but the youth team did a fantastic job of engaging in conversation and building rapport. A week later, they turned up again . . . and so did the police, to make the point that some of the young people were quite high on their watch list. Over the next fortnight, issues began to arise. Young people from

False Expectations

the church stopped going, and parents started talking. The pastor took the youth leader aside and raised the concerns, and the youth worker immediately re-launched the midweek discipleship groups, but with a real sense of empowering the young people to engage in reaching out to those beyond the church walls. But nothing could have softened the blow of what happened at the next youth club session. One of the girls had held it together long enough to get in, despite being high. 20 minutes later, she collapsed, having overdosed. The ambulance arrived quickly, and a crowd of young people gathered outside, angry that they weren't being allowed in. Police followed, but the damage was done. The window and doors could be boarded up, but not the mouths of the parents. Matty was exasperated.

"Andy, they will throw money at missionaries in Haiti, and send a team to minister to the migrants in Calais but they won't welcome young people on their doorstep who just need to know they are loved."

I feel his pain. But here's the problem: You want to be that mouthpiece of God's love but who, at the end of the day, is paying your wages, or footing the bill for the premises?

When I worked with an urban mission in the New Jersey, two board members from the church we partnered with gave us constant grief, be it over marks left on a table, the noise we created or some other issue that only they could see. Forget the fact that we were filling the building with over 50 children and young people from the neighborhood each week and creating strong ties with families that had no previous church connection. That said, there were moments of encouragement. On one occasion when a fellow intern and I were mopping the floor late into the evening, I was complaining about how the church never saw the amount we served them. No sooner were the words out my mouth than Hilary, our detractor-in-chief, walked in.

Hilary: "Oh, you're still cleaning."
Me: (look up, brace for sarcasm) "Sure thing."
Hilary: "We really appreciate your effort."
Me: "..."

We stood in stunned silence. Some approaches to youth work seem to cost so much more than others.

Back in the 90s Pete Ward suggested that most church based youth work is motivated by the parent's desire to keep church kids safe, and he identified a key difference between what he termed an *inside-out* and an *outside-in* approach to youth work.⁶ *Inside-out* starts with a core group and puts the onus on them to reach out to friends, through a mixture of attractional and relational events and programmes. This has been the model of choice for the majority of Christian youth work.

Conversely, *outside-in* starts at the rough edges, employing what we refer to as an incarnational approach, that is, following in Jesus' footsteps as he walked amongst the socially excluded and identified with the poor. While the journey starts beyond the boundaries, the path leads inwards, towards the church. Over the last two decades many projects and churches have pioneered successful *outside-in* youth work, although many acknowledge the toll to travel on this road is pricey. More recently, there has been the acknowledgement of a third way, that of *outside-out*, starting the journey miles from home, with no intention of navigating a way back. Outside is the new base camp.

Outside is the new *inside*.

I have empathy with those who want to kiss goodbye to the church and show them how it ought to be done. Two girls, no older than 14, walked into our morning service. I didn't recognize them from the community, and certainly knew that they were not part of any church youth group in the area, and my heart sank. You read that correctly. My heart sank. As lovely and as well-meaning as people were who said hello to them (we were a welcoming, family-orientated community), it was early days and we had no Christian youth presence to speak of, and at 25 I was the next oldest person to them in the congregation. I feared for them, that their first experience of church would either reinforce the image they already held, or that it would create one. Speaking to them before the service started, it emerged that they were just *trying it out*. I don't think they liked what they tasted. I didn't see them leave . . . or ever come back.

Let's say Sally successfully develops relationships out on the street and in the park with a number of young people. Is the end game for these young people simply to become pew fodder? Sally's church is not youth-ready, and she knows it. Her small group of 6 deeply committed Christian teens that meet on a Sunday would struggle immensely if just 2 young people from the park turned up. Increasingly, youth workers have become adept at working in all three categories, keeping them as distinct areas of practice.

---

6. See Ward, *Youthwork and the Mission of God*, 7-14, although Michael Eastman, founder of Frontier's Youth Ministry, had already articulated something of this in his book, *Outside In*.

Simultaneously, Sally encourages her home-grown young people to invite those they know to a Youth Alpha, yet spends time sitting with young people at the park, having deep God-conversations after 2 hours of basketball on the local court, watching the kingdom of God take root in young lives that she knows will never comfortably fit with even fresh expressions of church. One church that I worked with procured a new minibus, and promptly decked it out with the names of every church group. Across the back panel, "Something for everyone!" was splashed in the paint normally reserved for Joseph's coat. *"For everyone?"* I knew that even the diverse youth work I did hardly accommodated the spectrum of young people in the neighborhood. It was cringe worthy, but I understood the aspirational nature of the claim, and the heart of the pastor behind it.

Building from this lack of definition, the youth worker becomes a catchall for areas that need staffing. This used to be less apparent in statutory or voluntary work where funding influences and political agendas can drive the projects, and skill-set and age-range is often far narrower. I worked as a detached outreach worker for the council (outreach is interpreted a little differently by the Local Authority compared to the Church!) and the money came specifically from a funding stream targeting drug education. While my partner and I would drop in to youth clubs (normally for a quick cuppa), our work was otherwise exclusively on the streets, going to the places where we knew young people would hang out. We would engage groups and individuals, but specifically look to address situations and attitudes concerning drugs, signing off each location with a debrief and logging what had happened to help resource our future practice and identify trends. However, since the budget cuts began decimating the Youth Service, roles have been combined, mid-level managers removed and front-line jobs sacrificed.

The lack of definition can, however, be creative. Stop for a moment to think about boundaries. They actually work in two directions with several very different functions. Consider the school fence, designed to define the boundaries of the grounds, and not only keep dangers getting in, but also stop children escaping. There are also school gates that allow both controlled access and the ability to leave at the end of the day, much to the relief of teachers! Similarly, while boundaries need to be clear, they must not be too restrictive of creativity and potential partnership work, which will only occur if space is allowed. No coffee mornings tagged on to my work with the LA, but no space for serious creativity either. A friend of mine has survived a round of cuts to the Youth Service provision in his area, but his case load and role are now so narrow he is not allowed to pursue other avenues of youth work, except in his spare time.

LOOK AT WHO YOU ARE TREADING ON

I had finally opened Kenda Creasy Dean's book, *OMG: A Youth Ministry Handbook*, and was ploughing through it, when I hit chapter 4: *Promising Possibilities*, and suddenly became far more interested. She narrated the story of a neighborhood kid growing up in one of the toughest cities in the USA, who graduated from the afterschool programme to teen-leadership development, which earned him a University scholarship. Equipped with a degree, he returned to the city and became the ministry director in his old neighborhood. The thing is, I remember Albert—and his brother Tony, who didn't get a mention—and my heart was filled with a profound sense of joy and gratitude.[7] One of the sayings of *UrbanPromise*, the children's and youth organisation that I was involved with, was this:

"Work yourself out of the job."

The maxim was based on the belief that the best people to reach urban young people were not naïve white Brits like me, but Hispanic or African American men and women who had grown up in the city. Our youth development programme ran alongside the children's ministry and employed teens (many of whom had attended the children's ministry) to work as team members with us interns. The hope was that some would emerge as indigenous leaders and programme directors, but it is so often down to an intern or leader who saw something in them as they played basketball in the parks or painted faces at block parties.

Ever wondered why Jesus chose James and John? He didn't give them the nickname, *Sons of Thunder* for nothing. We can safely rule out the *Jerusalem Jalfrezi* and *Bethel Biryani*, and the associated proclivity for breaking wind—it was actually for their volatile and explosive manner. The gospels record several incidents where OTT fits the bill. Imagine wanting to obliterate a village for not offering a coffee when you stopped by to visit? James and John were a touch over-enthusiastic and certainly a long way off the finished article (Luke 9:52-56). I wouldn't have picked them for my team. Paul points out to the Corinthians that, "not many of you were influential,

---

7. I reached out to Albert and discovered he didn't actually know Kenda had written about him. Ironically, by naming him, she helped me connect the dots.

False Expectations

of noble birth or wise by human standards when you were called" (1 Corinthians 1:26). He goes on: "but God chose the foolish things of the world to shame the wise, the weak to shame the strong. He chose the lowly things of this world, the despised things, and the things that are not—to nullify the things that are." Why? "So that no-one may boast." And that's why Jesus picked them. In a crazy twist from the normal practice of Jewish rabbis who would have employed the first century equivalent of a sign-up sheet, Jesus hand-picked his disciples, calling James and John, along with 10 others, to "follow me."[8] He knew they would need intense discipling, and that he would be at times exasperated by them, but chose them anyway. "Discipleship such as Jesus demanded and inspired was apparently a new thing [. . .] something that did not fit in [. . .] with usual rabbinic customs or with customary rabbinic phenomena."[9] The evidence is powerful: When the Jewish leaders "saw the courage of Peter and John and realized that they were unschooled, ordinary men, they were astonished and they took note that these men had been with Jesus" (Acts 4:13). Jesus called those the world overlooked to accomplish his purposes "so that no one can boast" (Ephesians 2:9).

Weak youth leader needed. They are probably not far off. Would you self-identify as *a nothing*? As a failure? If you do, the journey is probably about to begin. God doesn't start with the finished article, but He's an expert when it comes to creating things *ex-nihilo*, out of nothing. I pick up on this theme of starting out from nothing, and handling failure in chapter 4, but suffice to say, equipped with a fresh vision of church and a simple framework to implement, you won't need a spider bite, genetic mutation or close encounter with bats to see God's kingdom come.

Looking for a Thor or a Superman to rescue the mission once again is big and bold, but their world is so different to ours. Bruce Wayne and Natasha Romanova, (aka Batman and Black Widow) on the other hand, are born and bred earthlings with hidden talent. If you have been doing youth work in a particular location for 5 years or more and have no-one coming through with leadership talent, however rough that diamond may appear, you need to reconsider your approach. Youth workers should be talent spotters, looking to raise up leaders from within to take their place. Check

---

8. Hull suggests 5 characteristics of 1st Century rabbinic discipleship, with the first as "deciding to follow a teacher" in *The Complete Book of Discipleship*, 63-4.

9. Montefiore, *Rabbinic Literature and Gospel Teaching*, 218. See also Young, *After the Fishermen*, 3.

under your soles—you may just have your foot on someone's face. But this principle should not simply apply to the worker. Churches and organisations that consistently hire from outside reduce the sense of opportunity and lower the motivation of those within. They do so sometimes because of burned fingers when they elevated someone in the past. It's risky business, as we explore in more detail in chapter 8, but the risks of bringing in a Thor far outweigh Peter, Bruce or Natasha. After all, the Thors know that *they did it better where they came from*, and it's out with the old, and in with the new. Unsurprisingly, we don't want another world—we want ours, albeit made new (Revelation 21:1-5). In the meantime, we see something of that future reality manifest through the church. Hiring from within reveals the hidden attributes of the body and reflects far better on the leadership than landing a flying star that may well wreak havoc in your atmosphere.

FOR REFLECTION AND DISCUSSION:

1. What has caused frustration in your role? How might you ease this tension?
2. What expectations are on you? How many of these are perceived? How many are clearly stated? How many are implicit?
3. Do you have a description of what you do? (this might be a job or role description)
4. How are you best rewarded? What motivates you to put in a shift?
5. Put the following into the order of what you prioritize when looking for a job (not all will apply, and some may be on a par with others):
    a. Pay
    b. Location
    c. Housing and package
    d. Family needs
    e. Job description
    f. Job title
    g. Level of challenge
    h. Provision of time off/further study
    i. Opportunities for growth

j. Denomination/ethos

CHAPTER ACTION POINTS:

1. Create dialogue with your line manager or pastor about what people expect of you, and what you expect of them. Sit down and review your original job description or role description over a coffee.
2. Set future review dates. If you do not do this, they most likely will not happen. Do the same for those who are on your team (volunteers, young leaders, etc.).
3. Do not shy from explaining how you work, what drives you, and what excites you about your ministry among young people.
4. If you are looking for a new worker, why not speak to a diocesan youth officer, the leadership of a church who have employed youth workers, or even a lowly lecturer in youth work to help tease out your thinking? This would best be done ultimately face to face in a consultancy fashion.

3

Mirrors = friends
Why self-reflection is so essential

LOOKING GOOD IN SPANDEX

WHAT DOES A SUPERHERO with a J on their chest look like?

Houston Heflin suggests that, "being a youth pastor requires skillfully juggling diverse roles in dissimilar contexts with people of multiple generations whilst enlisting others to join the effort. Paul recognized back in the first century this need for ministers to wear many hats."[1] He bases this on the passage where the apostle Paul writes that he has "become all things to all people" in 1 Corinthians 9:22; but pause for a moment to appreciate the context of the passage. Paul would do absolutely anything to see people come to know Jesus. In Romans 9:3, one of the most revealing and astounding passages in the New Testament, Paul writes, "I wish I myself were cursed and cut off from Christ for the sake of my Jewish brothers and sisters." It is very easy to read the Scriptures as a Westerner and strip the key players of their national identity. Doing that moves us into dangerous territory. Yet Jesus, Peter, and then Paul never denied their heritage, or their love for their Jewish family. Paul had not experienced much success amongst his kin, yet the gospel had exploded exponentially in Gentile (non-Jewish) circles to the extent that the Christian leadership of the time agreed that Paul was "an apostle to the Gentiles" (Galatians 2:8). Both in Rome and in Corinth, the majority of Christians were Gentiles, with a large Greek contingent in the

---

1. Heflin, *Youth Pastor*, 11.

latter, and it was critical that they understood that his end game was "to win as many as possible" (1 Corinthians 9:19).

Becoming all things is not in relation to spinning copious ministerial plates, but about creating bridges for the gospel with people in all sorts of settings and from any background. I love how King Agrippa recognizes this, asking Paul with a sense of incredulity, "Do you think that in such a short time you can persuade me to be a Christian?" Paul does not back down. "Short time or long—I pray God that not only you but all who are listening to me today may become what I am, except my chains" (Acts 26:28-29). Whilst Heflin's work is useful, in light of Paul's hugely influential work on the church, his premise looks rather like a proof-text if used to justify the spandex.

I'll let you into a secret.

Me: (Adopt chip on shoulder and suitably gruff voice) "I am Batman."

Personally, I can almost justify the outfit I bought on eBay. I have been described as *"God's Swiss Army Knife"* by a youth work veteran. Cool, right? Here is what I have learned about myself. It is true—I am seriously multi-talented. I can:

- Do the big-picture, blue sky vision-thing, yet get immersed in paying attention to detail (perfectionist tendencies),
- Design and create videos, promotional materials, websites, etc.,
- Drive things forward and "make things happen",
- Parachute into virtually any situation and do a decent job,
- Offer pastoral support, hear the heart cry, and relate to young and old across cultures,
- Lead worship (OK voice, 3 chords and the truth),
- Preach deep messages with rich application across the ages without people getting bored (it helps that I'm slightly ADHD myself),
- Create a sense of excitement, having great presence up front, whether it's running wide games or bouncing off the walls doing kids action songs,
- Approach a group of young people on the streets that I do not know and find ways in,

- Organize an orchestra in a Cornish tearoom, breakdance at parties, and do the admin that most youth workers detest, forget, ignore, or do badly.

Before you think I am either a plain-clothes Avenger or plain big-headed, you need to hear this: the trouble with a Swiss Army knife is that the blade is 2 inches long. I can almost hear Mick "Crocodile" Dundee from the 1980s cult classic of the same name looking at my offering, and saying through a smirk, "that's not a knife!" And then, as he brandishes his own 3-foot machete from behind his back, declaring, "now, *that's* a knife!"[2] The scissors can handle paper, but cannot remove the sleeves of my T-shirt. The screwdriver can tighten my aviators but happen upon a stubborn screw and it lacks the testosterone.

I need others around me. Soliciting feedback from my colleagues, one called me "fast-reactive," meaning I respond quickly, making assumptions about the situation. I can get things going, but my blinkered approach means I can miss key details and I lose impetus by myself. My pastoral support works well for one, but is alienating, or can be construed as cutting, to another. I do not always have the resources to get the job done after starting brightly. I am not the best small group leader. I misread how people feel in a situation. I'm sometimes surprised by a rising sense of anger that I simply have to quash before I turn green. My follow-through in public speaking needs work. I often get stuck on one thing, and sometimes go nowhere because of niggling fears and insecurities.

UNRAVELLING A COMMON THREAD

Back in the 90's Aiken called us to "drop the smooth omnicompetent leader image,"[3] and Pilavachi longed that, "The age of the all-singing, all-dancing, omni-competent, and perfect youth worker must finally come to an end,"[4] but the message is counter-intuitive, as correct as it may be. Our western Christian cultures propagate the hero-complex. I was once asked by a deacon, "Andy, do you think you are paid to release people, or paid to release people?" While my eyes glazed over, trying to understand what he was

---

2. Fairman, *Crocodile Dundee*, Rimfire Films, 1986.
3. Aiken, *Working with Teenagers*, 55.
4. Pilavachi, "The Vision," 24.

getting at, he was actually asking a critical question. Let me ask you the same question, only amplified:

"Are you in your role to empower others to get involved and use their individual gifts to serve the body of Christ, or are you used in the same manner as a domestic cleaner or gardener, to do the job with young people so that the church doesn't need to?"

In the middle and upper classes, *one* pays others to do the tasks *one* does not want to do, and on top of that, it is a sign of status, to have *one's* own gardener. We look for people to do the work for us, and if someone presents with an impressive array of skills, and we can afford them, they become our new star. This is not how the church should be. When youth ministry isn't owned by the church, it isn't surprising that the turnover of youth workers is high, as they are measured on their performance in conducting the jobs delegated to them.

Within 6 months of arriving at one church, over half of the volunteers had stepped down. I didn't take it personally, and I actually encouraged some of them to do so! They had been carrying the burden for so long with little training or support, and when paid backup arrived, they resigned, exhausted. In a different setting, we even had one top-quality couple give us 2 years notice! When does that happen in youth work? Both reflect people serving at arms-length from the body, without the strong sense of support and integration into the wider body, and lacking the cohesive vision producing passion for long term investment.

Some of the *"domestic cleaners"* and *"gardeners"* can believe their own hype. They have skills and aren't shy in showing them. I was at the induction service of a youth worker, who had left a previous church with some questions unanswered. The standout point for me was that he managed 15 minutes of interview in front of the church without saying one word about young people. We did learn, however, just how great he was! I wasn't surprised when I heard that he had moved on, less than a year into his tenure. He had all the charisma and ability in the world, save the one that should matter most: a passion for working with young people.

Creasy Dean identifies this as a "downside of professionalization [. . .] suggesting that faith formation is a job for professionals, not for families and communities." She recognizes, however, that "churches are beginning to recognize that youth ministry leadership must be shared by the entire congregation rather than assigned to one superhuman paid worker."[5]

---

5. Creasy Dean, *OMG*, 78.

While I share the desire for others to be involved, my contention is far more nuanced.

CALLING ALL REVOLUTIONARIES

Many people involved in youth work fit the description of Captain America and Black Widow –figuratively sporting proud symbols and aggressive tats, brandishing weapons and packing spandex: "just get us out there working with young people!" I have had numerous students get to the end of the second year of an undergrad degree and sense massive frustration that they still have a year left. The task is far more compelling than the theory, and we have learned through previous failures that planning is something to be endured as an unfortunate necessity if the event is going to be a success. However, our starting place should not be the battlefield itself, whether it is a military conflict, political arena, on the sports-field, or in the youth project.

Having played field hockey to a good standard, I knew the difference between turning out for the 4th team and for the 1st team. The 4th team just wanted to enjoy the sport (along with the pint and curry afterwards), and on many afternoons the team was cobbled together, involving numerous phone calls and arm-twisting. We would look around at the team at 3pm wondering which positions to combine with only 9 players (I sometimes had an HC alongside my name on the sheet—Headless Chicken—to cover defense, midfield and attack), elect a captain, throw together a few tactics based on the question, "where do you like playing?", and take to the pitch with 7 forwards! Conversely, on the 1st team we knew our positions, the formation we would employ, and we spent hours practicing short-corners so that when we won a *shortie* (the technical term!) all we had to do was call a number and execute the well-rehearsed play. We did not need to think about where to stand, having had it drilled into us until it was second nature. Yes, we could turn up and just play, but there was a far greater chance of success if we put in the hours planning and repeating the plays on the practice pitch.

So, action cannot be the starting place, but then, nor can planning. In the 2003 movie, *The Matrix: Revolutions*, the final instalment of the initial trilogy, Agent Smith confronts Mr Anderson (aka Neo) with the need for purpose:

"Illusions, Mr. Anderson. [. . .] The temporary constructs of a feeble human intellect trying desperately to justify an existence that is without meaning or purpose [. . .] You must know it by now. [. . .] It's pointless to keep fighting. Why, Mr. Anderson? Why? Why do you persist?"

Under duress Neo replies with the gutsy line that encapsulates the movie's philosophy . . .

"Because I choose to."[6]

Culturally, Neo opposes Smith's modernistic certainty with a post-modern, individualistic response that is the epitome of cool, but is completely vacuous. Yes, we have free will (distinguishing us from machines and giving us freedom to deny instinct) but it is incredibly nihilistic to do something for no reason whatsoever other than the ability to choose. When I challenged Stefan, 14, about why he stole his dad's car, I received a Neo-esque answer: "I just felt like doing it." I knew that those words were simply a mask, hiding the damaged relationships in his life. "I do it because I can" provides little meaning to the activity. Despite it being born out of his insecurities, even Spiderman had a reason for web-swinging across the cityscape in pursuit of criminals. Every year I ask youth work students why they do what they do, and the following are typical of the answers given:

- "I want to give back what others gave to me."
- "I love seeing the transformation and growth in young people."
- "I want them to have the opportunities that I never had."
- "I want to draw alongside them so that they know that they are never alone."
- "I want to share the love of God with them."
- "I love young people."
- "I want to be a role model for them."
- "I believe God has called me to work with teenagers."

The question scratches the surface of hidden motivations and deep convictions held by each one of us. We start with who we are, our assumptions, hopes and dreams. None of us are without bias or vested interest. Through the youth work training, I am involved in conscience-raising, helping students become more aware of self, others, and God.

6. The Wachowski Brothers, *Matrix Revolutions*.

"Why do I do what I do?"

This question is secondary to a more fundamental concept:

"Who do I think I am?"

These questions are critical to our practice. We can fall into two traps, believing either that we are better than we actually are, or not believing we are as good as we actually are. Romans 12:3 warns us not to "think of [ourselves] more highly than [we] ought to think, but to think with sober judgment, each according to the measure of faith that God has assigned." (ESV)

It is hard to teach this kind of self-awareness. I have found the Johari Window (named after its authors, Joe and Harry) an excellent heuristic for showing how to increase your awareness with a modified version included in Figure 6. It is an extremely flexible tool that many have developed over the years.

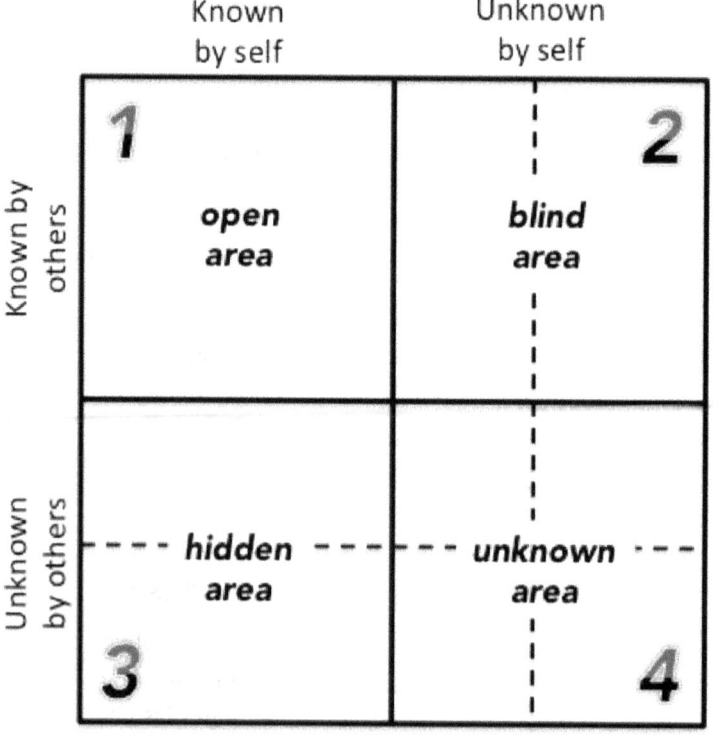

Figure 6: Johari Window[7]

7. Chapman, https://www.businessballs.com/self-awareness/

Quadrant 1 is your front stage. Everyone can see it, and you manage your performance with no surprises. However, there are characteristics that only others see in you, and Quadrant 2 can be marked by a lack of self, cultural or other-awareness. Emery-White helpfully points out that, "Personal spiritual practices alone are unlikely to shape young people to be like Christ. While necessary for growing in faith, they need to be embedded within other relationships, including participation in the church."[8] Why? Because it is hard to smell your own BO. Seriously. Both working with young people and with students, personal hygiene is one of those issues that can be extremely awkward and embarrassing to address, because the student can't detect the offensive odor that they live with 24/7. In the same way, being surrounded by others, held in supportive relationships, uncomfortable truths can be explored without shaming the individual.

In managing our front stage, Quadrant 3 illustrates that there are aspects of who you are that only you know. Embedded into trusting communities, we can allow others access back stage, and so, modelling for young people something many will not have ever seen or experienced. Capturing both Quadrant 2 and 3, the National Youth Agency note that, "When young people have a sense of belonging communities become stronger."[9] Emery-White points to the particular expression of church found in small groups, which he considers "vital because they provide the key values [. . .] of New Testament house churches: a sphere of intimacy, a place of mutual support, and a place of accountability."[10] One tension for the model is it struggles to handle multiple relationships in one go—no group has uniform knowledge of any single member, and it is natural to share to different levels depending on the context and individuals concerned. We are in good company. Jesus refused to be straight up with his brothers in John 7:2-9, had a core twelve, an inner three, "one whom he loved" (John 20:2), and chose to reveal himself first to women post-resurrection (Luke 24:10).

Quadrant 4 goes a step further, suggesting things that neither you nor any others know. While self-discovery and feedback from others can reduce the unknowns as is typically suggested, I believe that divine revelation and new experiences are absolutely critical to getting to grips with who we are.

johari-window-model-and-free-diagrams/ based on Luft and Ingham, *The Johari Window*.

8. Emery-White and Mackenzie, *Networks for Faith Formation*, 1.
9. NYA, in APPG, *Youth Work Inquiry*, 9.
10. Emery-White and Mackenzie, *Networks for Faith Formation*, 76-7.

"Would you still work with me if I never became a Christian?"

I gulped hard. The question penetrated the core of my evangelical commitments and probed my zest as an 18-year-old for seeing young people enter a relationship with Jesus that secures their eternity.

"Yes."

And I meant it. Until then, I had not been confronted with the underlying purposes of youth work or my own motivations. I had just got on with the task. In that moment, I realized that there was a bigger story than my own narrative. I started to understand that working with young people has something to do with wholeness. It's about nurture. And it demands my own integrity, especially before a holy God. Yes, we have "such a great salvation", but the Scriptures also call us to "remember the poor" (Galatians 2:10), to "look after orphans" (James 1:27), to usher in the kingdom of God, where, when fully realized, there will be no more tears, pain, suffering or death (Revelation 21:4).

Let's go beyond simply the sense of vocation, or calling, for the theologically-minded. Christians can get caught like rabbits in headlights when it comes to figuring out what we should do and what God is saying to us.

Josh trudged through the dining tent and plonked himself down next to me on a flimsy camping table. He was visibly upset.

Josh: "Why doesn't God speak to me?"

He had listened to the speaker on stage share an incredible story of being saved from a life of crime and abuse, a powerful call to ministry, and God seemingly now on speakerphone. In the response time, it felt as though everyone connected with God, while Josh heard only his own questions on endless repeat. Over the next 40 minutes, we explored his own hopes and dreams, his inner desires and motivations. I opened up the story of Abram in the pages of Genesis. On the surface, it seemed like Abram lived from one epic moment to the next, but a closer reading reveals that Abram was 75 when he heard *the call*. For 75 years Abram had lived a very normal life, with nothing to suggest he was well connected, or that he even knew God. He experiences enforced displacement when a famine hits the land, and chapters 15 and 16 of Genesis detail the call and Abrams subsequent drama. Chapter 16 ends with the birth of Ishmael, and chapter 17 kicks off with a fresh promise from God. Note that 13 years pass from one verse to the next. Thirteen!

Me: "Josh, that's like, 80% of your life! Nothing but a deep silence from the Almighty."

I love how Creasy Dean captures it: "In truth, discerning our vocation is a lifelong process with dramatic results but a lot less day-to-day drama."[11] When I haven't *received* revelation, I go back to what I do know about myself, my understanding of Scripture, my commitments, my personality and wiring, and I move out from there.

ONE BODY, MANY PARTS

Once we have established something of our own motivation and sense of self, we need to ask whether it is consistent with bigger vision and motivation of the church or organisation. I can guarantee either a short tenure, or years of frustration if this matching process doesn't take place. That's why many churches request prospective youth workers to come and spend a weekend with the church. For me, even a weekend isn't enough.

Sam felt like she was banging her head on a brick wall at her placement church. She shared that her heart was breaking for the young people who were best when they were "seen and not heard" from what she had experienced. She wondered aloud whether she should commit her final year of college to developing something there. My answer caught her off-guard. I said I could guarantee a year of frustration, metaphorically building what would be a small pile of rocks next to a well-constructed house. When the year was over, the church would not think twice about knocking the rocks over and leveling it out again. The church did not own the youth work, and I doubted they even knew why they wanted it in the first place. When the vision for the youth ministry is at odds with that of the church, there is only one winner.

My vision for body ministry begins to be teased out here. Others have seen me as the bridge for the gospel to travel from the Christian tradition and church to the young people *out there*, yet I do not see myself in that way. My motivation is to enable everyone to play their part. If I am insecure in who I am, I will start to dance to the tunes others play, and experience disappointment when I fail to meet their expectations.

---

11. Creasy Dean, *OMG*, 103.

STARTING RIGHT...

We do things for a reason, and for Christians, working with young people should be a profoundly theological task. But why start with theology? Why not from philosophy, or out of anthropological concern? As Christians we believe that a two-part question *precedes* the issue of our identity, articulated by my Christian Doctrine lecturer from my college days, Dotha Blackwood:

"What kind of God... and so what?"

God has revealed something of Himself. We only know God by what He has revealed, and it is this creative act that underpins theology. Andy Root contends that "good ministry leads to good theology [...] Ministry always precedes theology and becomes the fodder for constructive theological thought because of our claim that God is living and active in the world—which means that God is a Minister." He concludes that, "Theology is nothing more than reflecting on God's action"[12] and Creasy Dean adds that "all decent theology begins and ends in practice."[13] These go a little too far: God reveals His character through speech as much as action. Think about the proclamation in Exodus 34:6, "the Lord, the Lord, compassionate and gracious God, slow to anger, abounding in love and faithfulness." This is not an egotistical deity in need of affirmation, but clear explication of who He intrinsically is. My concern here is that we do not lose sight of the primary location for our theology: The Bible.

It is here that we see God revealed most clearly. C.S. Lewis argues that "if you do not listen to Theology, that will not mean that you have no ideas about God. It will mean that you have a lot of wrong ones."[14] We see in the Scriptures how God allows us to understand His nature, through use of narrative, prophecy and poetry. I love what are called *anthromorphisms*—human characteristics attributed to God so that we can begin to relate and make sense of ideas so much bigger than ourselves. Does God really have, what Numbers 6:24 calls, a shiny face? As Psalm 33:6 suggests, does breath come out of His mouth, if He has one? And does God scatter His enemies, as Psalm 89:10 indicates, with His mighty arm? And what of the wings in Psalm 57:1 and Malachi 4:2?

---

12. Root, *The Theological Turn*, 40.
13. Creasy Dean, "Theological Rocks," 36.
14. Lewis, *Mere Christianity*.

Anthromorphisms are ultimately put aside when God revealed Himself in the person of Jesus of Nazareth, as the Christmas carol expresses so concisely:

> "Veiled in flesh the God head see
> Hail the incarnate Deity
> Pleased as man with man to dwell
> Jesus our Emmanuel"[15]

We cannot ascend to where God is. He must descend and make Himself known on our level, so Scripture must take precedence over tradition, culture and our own stories. I am indebted to my colleague, Colin Bennett, for his STOP model that challenges a number of more contextualized *flat* models by prioritising the Bible:[16]

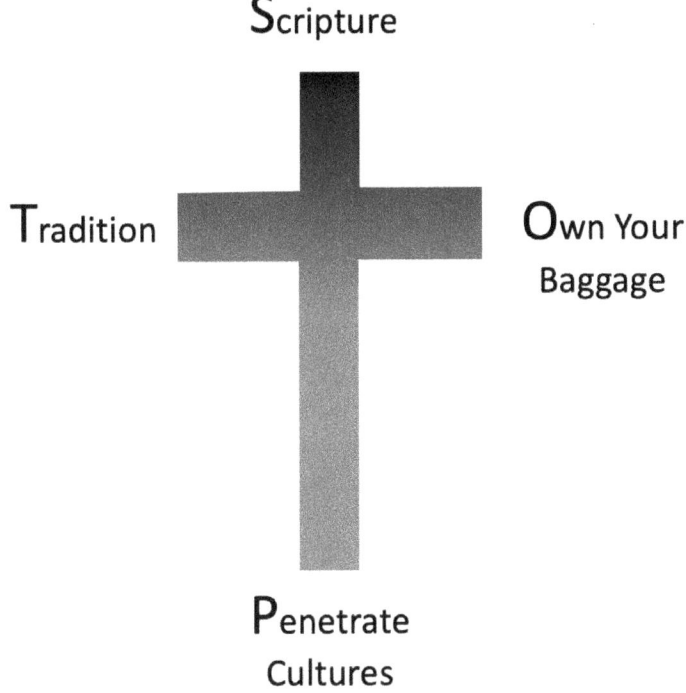

---

15. I'm not a fan of many Christmas Carols, with some nonsensical theology out there, but Charles Wesley's *Hark the Herald Angels Sing* published in 1739 contains this articulate summary of the incarnation.

16. I originally provided the artwork for the model, referenced in various texts, including Bennett, "Working with Families," 212-3.

Figure 7: STOP Before you Start: Towards an Applied Theology

Starting with the bible does not mean finding a verse to support your point. That's called proof-texting, and as one of my lecturers used to say, "A text without a context is a pre-text for a proof-text." We must handle the Word of God correctly (2 Timothy 2:15), as McGonigal notes, "The Bible has a lot to say about youth, although not in exactly the same context as implied in the modern term adolescent. This distinction illustrates the essential principle of biblical interpretation that original cultural setting is primary, and application into contemporary situations is secondary."[17] Understanding as best as we can what the authorial intention was provides some protection from making the bible fit your own narratives. "[Christian] Youth work is only as good as its underpinning theology,"[18] and STOP forces us to wrestle first with what God has revealed in the Bible, before then drawing on Tradition, understanding our personal narrative in Owning your baggage, and taking account of the environment around us in Penetrate Cultures.

In their brilliant and concise title, *Who Needs Theology?* Grenz and Olson suggest there are two key tasks for theology: the critical and the constructive.[19]

The Critical Task . . .

explores and evaluates beliefs and teachings about God, the world, and ourselves. This is done in light of the Bible and secondary Christian sources, and correlates to Bennett's first heading, and I would want to sharpen it up by asking very simply, what does the bible say about young people, ignoring our culture, & contemporary reading?

The Constructive Task . . .

develops models of biblical teaching, connecting the dots to our cultural contexts. Out of this second task emerges theological themes, which underpin much of our practice. Again, I would suggest that we ask, based on our answers to the previous question, how does the bible inform our practice

---

17. McGonigal, "Focusing Youth Ministry", 125-6.
18. Savage et al., *Making Sense of Generation Y*, 129.
19. Grenz and Olson, *Who Needs Theology?* Ch5.

today? This will lead to creative, contextualized responses to the issues we face, yet ones that are as faithful as possible to the "ancient Christian message"[20] and the biblical text.

While so much has been written on incarnational ministry, it is a contested concept, and just one theological strand in Christian youth work as we have seen. Outside-in models, as we will discover, can lead to high relational support of individuals, but low personal or spiritual challenge. This is far removed from the way Jesus went about ministry, and growth can emerge incredibly slowly. More on that later. There are other themes, such as discipleship, worship, evangelism, mission and service. There are also our understandings of the person and work of the Holy Spirit, God as Father, the theology of adoption, and so on, all of which contribute to our ecclesiology.

It's time to lose the spandex and get to know not just who we are, but whose we are. We might just find that our youth work is richer as a result.

FOR REFLECTION AND DISCUSSION:

1. If you were to use a human analogy, how would you describe God? (Head teacher, Robin Hood, Police Officer, etc.) What does this analogy communicate—about God and about you?
2. How has your experience shaped your perception of God and what He is like?
3. I contend that the three tasks of adolescence articulated by Chap Clark are as relevant in your 20s, 30s . . . or even 80s as they were in your teens. Pause to reflect. How would you answer these?
   - Who am I?
   - Do I matter?
   - How do I relate to others?[21]

CHAPTER ACTION POINTS:

Go back to the Johari Window (Figure 6). Make a plan for your own growth using the following as a starter.

20. Morris, *Flexible Church*, 7.
21. Clark, "The changing face of Adolescence," 55.

Quadrant 2: Blind Area

Ask those around you, especially those who you might struggle a little with, to give you written feedback. Use headings such as: How do I handle pressure? What are my strengths in relation to . . . .? and What one thing would you change about me?

Assess the feedback. Are there any surprises? Do you agree/disagree?

Quadrant 3 Hidden Area

Be selective, but plan to share more deeply and practically. Do your team know that you are a little obsessive about the dishes left in the kitchen sink? Would the church benefit from hearing about how you tick? Rather than gloss over failure, would the young people appreciate sharing some of your disappointment? (Remember, some of them can only see your gadget belt . . .)

Quadrant 4: Unknown Area

My old principal at Bible College, Steve Brady, had a brilliant rule of thumb regarding time out: "Divert Daily, Withdraw Weekly, Abandon Annually." These times for your own quietness and reflection are sources of strength, and it is often in prayer and solitude that we discover new things about ourselves and the God we serve.

4

Zombies are Biblical

How to start from scratch

Would you rather own the Bat Cave or Stark Tower? It's a tension. Batman's secret bunker is built underneath a mansion, accessed in numerous ways, including via a depressed F# on his piano, while Ironman's pad is obnoxious in its display of wealth and status. What unites the two is that they didn't just happen. Bruce Wayne's journey into the darker areas of his own life led him to begin work on the South East corner of Wayne Mansion, and Tony Stark's billions started life in the sweat and toil of his grandad's workshop. It's what I loved as a child—and adult—about Lego. You don't buy a Lego model that is already constructed, and you can't buy an off-the-shelf body for Christ, either. In this chapter, we will be exploring what it looks like to start from scratch, or as close to it as possible.

Question: If you were going to serve at a church that had no student ministry program, where would you begin?

Josh Griffin, High School Pastor of Saddleback Church (think *Purpose Driven Church*) answered that on his blog by saying he would first "build a crack team of volunteers." Secondly, he states that, "the first program [he] would launch is a worship service." The ministry would, "Begin with a simple program that is relationship-focused, friendly to outsiders and builds a community. It'll give you a great base to build on from there!"[1]

---

1. Griffin, "Q&A: Starting a Youth Ministry from Scratch."

I want to get excited with him and given a nucleus-fringe approach in a medium to large US church it can work, but the model and methodology do not translate into small US churches, let alone the UK church culture.

Problem, number one: Aside from the rehab program needed for your *crack* volunteers (bad joke, sorry!), building an all-star team before kick-off is a pipe-dream in the typical UK church, and high-quality players are unlikely to emerge or sign up in your first couple of seasons.

Problem, number two: There are no teens. Phoebe Thompson, the first head of the Youthscape Centre for Research, provided a reality check by profiling Luton, a town north of London with a population of 258,000, 22,000 of whom are young people. She revealed that in 2016 there were approximately 100 churches in Luton, and a staggering 75% had no youth work.[2] So for every church that had a youth ministry, there were 3 that do not. And I am told that Luton is above average.

Tina and Nathan were the only teenagers at the church that Steve, a friend of mine, led. Each week was a battle, being dragged along by their parents. At 16, Tina exercised her right to stop going—her mum realising it wasn't worth the fight.

Josh Griffin: "Steve, why don't you kick off with a worship service, or perhaps a youth group?"

Steve: "Sorry, Josh, but one is not a group."

What can I contribute to this area? Martin Saunders wrote an excellent step-by-step manual with many ideas and broad perspectives, titled, Youth Work from Scratch[3] and I recommend it as further reading. However, this chapter has emerged from a seminar I gave at *Youthwork: The Conference* back in 2012, riding on the back of personal experiences of being heavily involved in building up several youth works in a Christian context. The first was a satellite programme of a significant urban ministry launched into a new city; the second was an inherited work out of which we launched new expressions of youth work; and the third almost completely from scratch, although there had been a vibrant open access club run for many years out of the church, but with no Christian conversion or discipleship emerging. Out of this, and many conversations with youth workers, and observations that I have made now as a youth work trainer, I want to ask one critical

---

2. Phoebe Thompson, *Youthscape Centre for Research launch event*, 15th February 2016.

3. Saunders, *Youth Work from Scratch*.

question, then, pending your answer, offer three encouragements and three principles for starting out.

QUESTION: WHY DO YOU WANT TO START A YOUTH WORK?

A colleague and I were asked by a church leader whether there was potential for a student to be placed with them. We talked through the options, and when we mentioned youth work, the leader seemed to experience an epiphany:

"A youth worker! I'd never thought of that. We could do with someone in that area."

We explored this with them and discovered that the aging church did not actually have any teens involved in any expression of its existence. So why start from scratch?

Churches can feel compelled to do youth work, as if it is the must have ministry, and status can be found in possessing a thriving youth project. It can also be the arm of the church most acceptable to local authorities. A church I know had a MUGA (Multi-Use Games Area) installed by the council on their facilities because of the scale of the youth work being done by the church. In one setting, the local women's football team raised money to resource our church youth work with equipment, and the parish council regarded us as the most consistent and effective youth work in the area. Other churches are simply aware that the future of their denomination depends on investing in youth work, but I want to make this personal: what's your vision?

One of my favorite definitions of vision is "a picture of the future that produces passion,"[4] and this drive is what will keep you going when the inevitable hard times come. The disciples saw a glimpse of the kingdom of God in a tradesman and gave up their day-jobs to follow the unconventional rabbi. They "caught a vision—a dangerous, obsessive, and wonderful epiphany that has captured hearts ever since."[5] Like the disciples, while vision is caught person by person, the roll out is corporate, and found in body ministry. Youth work is not meant to be a solitary adventure, and your vision needs to gain traction in community. Start communicating it in conversations around the table, in the small group, at church and at the school

4. Hybels, *Courageous Leadership*, 33.
5. Greig, *The Vision and the Vow*, pxx.

gates and don't let up. Covey provides us with our mantra: "The main thing is to keep the main thing the main thing."[6]

ENCOURAGEMENT NUMBER ONE: WHATEVER YOU'VE HEARD, IT'S NOT GOING TO WORK.

"Do not attempt to copy any of the moves described in this book. They have been performed by a complete novice masquerading as a professional, and have cost everything . . ."

That would make an awesome opening to a "how to" manual, but I doubt anyone will start in that way. Instead we read:

"Follow the steps we took. Embrace the processes we proved in building this ministry. Align your ministry with our Bible-centered approach, rebrand your product, and it will sell."

Here is the problem with the how to approach: It's not faith; it's actually more akin to magic. There are rafts of magic books in Christian circles, and self-help is preached far too often from pulpits. If you need an example, consider self-esteem. On one level, with so many insecurities around body image propagated by the media, sessions on building self-esteem seem well placed, and there are a number of Bible verses that seem to speak into this area. However, the overwhelming message in the New Testament is to "die to yourself" (Galatians 2:20), "reckon yourself dead" (Romans 6:11), and "hate your life" (John 12:25)! The problem with discovering self-esteem is that you need a self that you can esteem! Some people can find little of worth, but the Christian message is recognising that "you have died, and your life is now hidden with Christ" (Colossians 3:3). I can esteem the person of Jesus, and I have discovered that it is Christ in me that gives me worth (Colossians 1:27).

No offence to the plethora of authors out there, but there is only one book for Christian youth workers: the "Complete Book of Youth Ministry"[7] (granted, it was written in the 1980s). The self-help genre sells bestsellers because we *like* formulas, and we *want* results. Off the shelf answers might provide a quick fix, but they can squeeze spirituality out and ignore the nuances and complexities of your particular situation. If you want a faith-full ministry, prepare for hard graft, but rest in the assurance that your faith pleases God (Hebrews 11:6).

6. Covey, *The 8th Habit*, 160.
7. Senter and Benson, *The Complete Book of Youth Ministry*.

Having done more than my fair share of children's work, often from the premise of working with children transitioning up into youth work, or with the teens who are helping out, I know that they will often give you the answer that they think you want. "Jesus is the answer - now what's the question?" Christian youth work must move away from the pat answer and do the hard work of working through the presenting issues and those that lie beneath. "Jesus is not the answer"—you heard it first here—"He's the question." Jesus asks questions of us and calls into question our motives and desires. How are you going to be Jesus to these young people? How far are you willing to go to raise a shout for Him? Jesus challenged,

> "Anyone who loves their father or mother more than me is not worthy of me; anyone who loves their son or daughter more than me is not worthy of me. Whoever does not take up their cross and follow me is not worthy of me. (They are not worthy to be my disciple. Luke 14:26) Whoever finds their life will lose it, and whoever loses their life for my sake will find it." (Matthew 10:37-39)

Jesus is the question.

ENCOURAGEMENT NUMBER TWO: NO ONE WILL THINK BADLY OF YOU IF YOU QUIT NOW.

Thomas Alva Edison, eventual inventor of the light bulb, is reputed to have said in the face of criticism, "I have not failed. I've just found 10,000 ways that won't work." It's hard to deal with failure in any sphere, let alone in youth work. If I knew what the personal cost would be to being a pastor or a youth worker before signing up, I may have had second thoughts. My first taste of failure was in the inner city, working with Omar, a 14-year-old African American. He was street-smart and seemed to have been born with the kind of chiseled physique that any track star would have to work tirelessly for. We employed him as a role model and mentor, alongside many other urban teens, to work with younger children in the after-schools clubs and activity programmes, and he played in our basketball start-up initiative. Employment in the inner city is a big deal and being part of the programme enables teenagers to access opportunities that they would not otherwise be exposed to. One spring-time afternoon he was working with an 8-year-old student on a Mathematics challenge. The hypnotic sound of a dozen HB leads criss-crossing sheets of paper was severed by the snapping in two of the pencil in Omar's hand. The children stared in disbelief and some fear as stationary took to flight across the room along with angry curse words, before Omar grabbed his coat and left - the door hinges barely surviving the exit. In a modern-day recreation of Luke 15's parable, I left the 99 children untended and left in hot pursuit of the lost kid, although what Jesus failed to detail was what happens if the pursuer is on foot and the pursued on a BMX. I eventually caught him within a mile of the church campus, and he spoke over my gasping and panting for air:

Omar: "Andy, that's me done. I don't want it no more. Just forget about it."

The problem was, I couldn't. He verbally underscored his decision, yet he could not give me a clear or compelling reason why. I tried to meet up with Omar over the following weeks, but he became elusive, disconnected from the programme and even his peers. We managed to piece together the reason why he left so abruptly: he found himself frustrated and emasculated by the fact that at 14 he did not have the academic ability to help children half his age with their homework. Four months later I spotted Omar on his BMX with a girl perched on his back. He told me she was pregnant. I went for the commitment issue immediately—would he stick with her, etc., to which he made the right noises. The next I heard he was with a different girl and running the streets for a dealer. Statistically, the future wasn't looking good for him.

Since Omar, there have been many young people who I have seen fall through the cracks in the programming, and drop through the safety net of relational work, and each one is significant. Unlike in sports, there is no practice ground for youth work and ministry. I had the privilege with my 6th form 1st-XI hockey team to take on Wales U18 before they participated in a home-nations tournament. We drew with two goals apiece, however, the results will never be listed in the Welsh history annals. The exercise was preparation for the real thing. Here's our problem: you cannot play warm-up matches in youth work. Even when you are a student, the placements are for real, and the lives you impact with your decisions, your selfish attitude, your bad mood, are flesh and blood.

Each apparent failure should make you stop to reflect. To what extent was I at fault? Would any other course of action have led to a different result? Those with reflective personalities will find this more natural than others, but even action-junkies like me need to pause in order to reflect if we are going to get anything out of our failures.

So, I give you permission right here and right now, to bow out gracefully. Saunders is right—you don't get into youth ministry for the money, the fame or the glory.[8] In fact, this youth work thing will cost you far more than you can imagine at the start. Why? In the words of the late Mike Yaconelli, co-founder of Youth Specialties, "Real ministry is not what you do, but who you are."[9] Get this wrong even when you are doing things right may even cost you your soul.

ENCOURAGEMENT NUMBER THREE: START WITH WHAT YOU HAVE, BUT BELIEVE . . .

Youth work from scratch is never *"ex nihilo"*, out of nothing. That's God's domain. Perhaps it would be more accurate to call the subject, *"Revitalising youth work"*. Starting out from scratch isn't out of nothing, ever. It refers to a line chalked on the floor a few feet in front of the starting line of a race, for runners who would nowadays turn up at the Paralympics. Blades don't need a head start. Ask Oscar.[10] You may see nothing happening at a church (and there are at least 59% of churches without 15—19 year olds),[11] but communities possess memory, and what may seem like the mess of a maternity ward as you birth something new, is actually built over a graveyard. But the way I see it, God has a habit of breathing new life into old, dry bones. Or, perhaps more controversially, *into zombies*.

The prophet Ezekiel is taken in a vision to a valley carpeted by sun-bleached human carcasses. Ceremonially, he would have been considered unclean, but that is in some respects a moot point. So what. The bones represent the Israeli people (Ezekiel 37:11) and the question is posed:

God: "Son of man, can these bones live?"

The answer is pained, stripped of any pride or pretence:

Ezekiel: "O sovereign Lord, only you know!"

Ezekiel is told to prophesy to the bones, and, accompanied I'm sure by Transformer-esque sound effects, an army stands to its feet, muscle-bound

---

8. Saunders, *Youth Work From Scratch*, 13.
9. Yaconelli, *Getting Fired for the Glory of God*.
10. Although he will be forever remembered for being convicted of killing his girlfriend in 2013, Oscar Pistorius, who at 11 had both feet amputated, overcame incredible opposition to win the legal right to race against able-bodied runners—and secured a silver with the SA 4x400m team.
11. Brierley, "Where is the church going?"

and clothed with skin. Yet the forms are still lifeless. Enter our zombie-hunter-turned-theologian, Joseph Blenkinsopp, who observes that, "the narrative is held together by the key term, ruah. It occurs ten times [and] can be translated "spirit," "breath," or "wind.""[12] Ezekiel is then told to speak to this ruah, to "give life to this array of zombies [in] a reenactment (sic) of the primal act of creation."[13]

While a number of commentators use this passage to advocate life after death, it is really about "the divine work of [recreation . . .] through the prophetic word and Spirit."[14] A friend of mine who runs his own successful business has a saying that acts as a reality check:

"We are as we are, and it is as it is."

We start with what we have, but trust that God will breathe life into the lifeless, "being sure of what we hope for, and certain of what we do not see" (Hebrews 11:1). Look at the statistics, or make it personal and think about Keli, a promising girl in our youth group, but one beset by chaotic family life and surrounded by negative influences on her estate. Pregnant at 14 to what I can only call a dangerous 18-year-old lad, she has since had her children removed from her to join the ever-increasing number of children in care in the UK, which stood at over 75,000 in 2018.[15] Despair and cynicism is the easy response; being part of the solution is the right response. As Christians, we call on a God who breathes life, while we walk in step-by-step obedience, acting justly and loving mercy (Micah 6:8).

There are variants to this saying, but people generally over-estimate what they can do in a year, and underestimate what they can achieve in four. I got this wrong in my earlier days, believing that big events equal big results. It just doesn't hold true. As a church we spent several thousand pounds on an outreach event. I tip my beanie to former Christian hip-hop group, *The 29th Chapter*, who didn't just come and do a gig on a flat-bed truck in the middle of a field in the Chilterns, but spent over an hour post-event sitting and talking with unchurched young people. I will never know the long-term impact of that event, but I do know and can measure some things. I know that there were just over 100 young people who had no

---

12. Blenkinsopp, *Ezekiel*, 173.

13. Blenkinsopp, *Ezekiel*, 173.

14. Duguid, *Ezekiel*, 430.

15. The UK Government recorded 75,420 looked after children in 2018, a 10% increase from 2014. See https://www.gov.uk/government/statistics/children-looked-after-in-england-including-adoption-2017-to-2018.

obvious connection to church in attendance. I know that we did not add a single young person to our small groups (some which were composed of 75% unchurched young people), nor did I have any further contact with the 7 or 8 who made first time "professions of faith".

If I compare that event with the consistent, weekly groups that met in our home, it is not difficult to say which was more effective.

I knew we were succeeding when I posed this question:

"What is the most significant decision you have ever made?"

As we made our way around the packed room (6 young people to every 3-seater), I anticipated that maybe 50% would say that it was in becoming a Christian. What I did not expect was the number of them that said that the biggest decision they have ever made was "to live out my faith in front of my friends." That takes tenacity, courage, and resilience. That takes the *ruah* of God.

Having moved on after seven years in that area, I still see many of those young lives walking the narrow path, whether they have gone on to Christian training or ministry, or pursued a career in architecture, finance, home-making, the forces or the arts, committed to the embodiment of faithful service and Christian love.

> "There was no single defining action, no grand program, no one killer innovation, no solitary lucky break, no wrenching revolution. Good to great comes about by a cumulative process—step by step, action by action, decision by decision, turn by turn [. . .] that adds up to sustained and spectacular results." Collins cynically adds, "to read media accounts [. . .] you might draw an entirely different conclusion."[16]

My role is simple: keep on keeping on in the small things, faithful in speech and action, leaving the resurrection of the dead to God.

PRINCIPLE NUMBER ONE: PARTNERSHIPS: IF THEY ARE NOT AGAINST YOU, THEY ARE FOR YOU

In Luke 11:23 Jesus is recorded as saying that, "Whoever is not with me is against me." It's a polarizing verse that points to taking sides, and, along with Scriptures such as Paul's injunction not "to team up with those who are unbelievers" in 2 Corinthians 6:14 (NLT), Churches and Christian

---

16. Collins, *Good to Great*, 165.

groups have been persuaded to keep themselves to themselves, and do their own thing.

In one church tradition, I was told that this was a prohibition stretching to not working with churches if they were not *gospel* churches, lest the message be somehow compromised. This arrogant sectarianism is guilty of lazy exposition. Scroll back just two chapters to Luke 9:49-50, and we read of an encounter that the disciples had with another group.

"Master," said John, "we saw someone driving out demons in your name and we tried to stop him, because he is not one of us."

"Not one of us." In their naivety, the disciples utter the words that sit at the heart of divisions, whether between rival schools, church denominations, political parties, and world powers. Jesus obliterates their resistance:

"Do not stop him, for whoever is not against you is for you."

Is Jesus contradicting Himself in the space of two chapters? Context here is critical. In the latter, the discussion is centered on the big picture, heaven vs. hell, good vs. evil, with one commentator brilliantly noting, "There are no Switzerlands in this cosmic war."[17] In contrast, the earlier passage challenged the notion of who's in and who's out. Swindoll writes that, "Jesus used this opportunity to reorganize the disciples' organizational chart."[18]

In a small village context, there was little choice. Either work with churches that may perhaps be more liberal or think differently than you or work alone. It was made pretty clear that partnerships should only be with other *gospel* churches. Their criteria for such a church ruled out several on our doorstep in the rural area. In a larger town or bigger city, such as the sprawling conurbations of Birmingham or Manchester, you can get away with that position and still look like you work with others. Christians are so often known for what they are against, and so rarely for what they are for. I think this is why the psalmist wrote "how blessed it is when brothers dwell together in unity, for there the Lord commands a blessing" (Psalm 133), because it is plain hard work to work through differences and yet still be brothers and sisters.

We made the choice to work closely with churches that differed on matters of nuanced theology . . . and less so. There were lay preachers who did not believe in the reality of Hell, for example, where our church was much more reformed in belief. If you are that passionate about the differences,

---

17. Bock, "Why Miracles."
18. Swindoll, *Insights on Luke*, 247.

partner anyway! You will be more likely to influence them when they are embraced rather than held at arm's length. Our Christian youth work started in ecumenical partnership, not in some dogmatic or contractual form, but through covenantal relationship. With just two Christian teens in my local church, we knew we needed more to achieve critical mass, so we started a conversation with other churches in the area. To this day I valued my friendship with Charlotte, a Methodist minister who joined in the work with us. We did not ignore or diminish our theological differences, in fact, one of the richest sessions was when we hosted a forum for the young people to explore these differences yet see the common threads that united us. To reduce the sense of territorialism and the evident nervousness that we as the more trendy church might steal sheep, we began our meetings in the Methodist chapel *snug* rather than locate the youth work in our buildings, and the growth we saw affirmed the truism that, "it is amazing what you can accomplish if you do not care who gets the credit."[19] This sent out a clear sign, and reminded me how important location is, as Smith helpfully says, "meeting somewhere that avoids one group feeling more at home than another."[20]

I have been privileged to work with Helen Hender as she pioneered what is now the Bournemouth and Poole Youth Network, which draws together as many as 40 youth workers from across the conurbation for prayer, support and strategic planning. We have discovered that many youth pastors, youth workers and volunteer leaders are not aware of, let alone have met, those even around the corner, who are doing the same kinds of ministry, drawing young people from the same catchment area. Youth workers have far too closely mirrored the often-parochial outlook of their church leaders, who build *their* churches (a distortion of Matthew 16:18) rather than seek first *His* kingdom (Matthew 6:33). Para-church and independent youth works are often highly nervous of partnering with churches, suspicious (sometimes rightly) that the leaders want to *own* them and institutionalize their movement.

If we cannot work through our differences with other Christian traditions and start to do some joined up thinking, what hope do we have working with non-Christian organisations, who may share something of our desire to see God's kingdom come, even if they do not use the same language? Partnership outside of the Christian faith can actually increase

---

19. This is attributed to Harry S Truman, 33rd president of US (1884—1972).
20. Smith, "Inclusive Theology," 90.

your opportunities for Christian mission and should not be feared. Andy Burns has some helpful advice, suggesting that we first own our mission, recognize our personal drivers, and focus on what unites those at the table.[21] I make no apology for sounding like a song on repeat: don't lose sight of, compromise, or let go of that God-given vision, and partnership has a strong chance of being sweet. Allow the main course to become a side dish, and partnership will become sour.

PRINCIPLE NUMBER TWO: IDENTIFY AND BUILD STRONG LINKS WITH YOUR STAKEHOLDERS

One of the most important tasks of youth work in the early days is to work out who has an interest in your success and the work being done. These may or may not see themselves as stakeholders, but upon identification, they should be treated as such. Why? Because they will be the ones championing your cause when negative press circulates behind closed doors (which it will), and they are the ones who will demonstrate their commitment in areas where it matters most, such as buildings, projects and finances (which it often does).

The English medieval proverb encourages us to "make hay while the sun shines," and the farmer who delays may just find no one willing to lend a hand when the skies cloud over and the grass is sodden. Granted, most of us have no intimate knowledge of arable life, but many know about intimate relationships. The early days are full of romance. Personal foibles that might be crass are seen as cute, and mannerisms that could disgust somehow delight. There is no pressure of engagement, or commitment of marriage, and you talk for hours sharing random oddities and endless *top ten* lists. Date the stakeholders. Drop in *just for a coffee* with one of the elders of the church, turn up at the local festival and chat with the community organizers, take the councilor out for lunch to listen to her vision for the area.

But at some point, the question drops, dating stops and the champagne pops. Engagement and marriage formalize a relationship, and stakeholders need to know what their relationship with you entails. That can be articulated on paper or simply a verbal handshake, but the desire is for clarity all round.

---

21. Burns, "Partnership working... from scratch," 111.

Once wed, no one wants to live with a couch potato who doesn't lift a finger to help, taking the promises uttered before friends, family and a Father in heaven for granted. The relationship must be invested in, with PDAs (Public Displays of Affection) and random acts that say, "I love you". But more than that, for this relationship to avoid stalemate, there needs to be more than the flowers and chocolate after a month of silence. At the core of our relationship with our stakeholders, there needs to be constant lines of communication. Nobody with a vested interest in a work wants to hear about critical events second or third hand. Involve your stakeholders and create mechanisms for updates and keeping your vision in their gaze. Nowhere better was this seen than the team of people involved in the Slum Survivor project that we ran, where we achieved coverage from national news on two occasions, and the reason for this was our intentionality about engaging those who supported our work in some way during the planning process. It is easy to tell when you are an after-thought.

Sometimes, you can draw volunteers from your stakeholders, the obvious one being church members, if you are attached to a local body. Clearly Saunders and I have had different experiences of recruitment, and I would discourage the upfront notice for volunteers in favour of the hand-on-shoulder approach. [22] Public notices often seem desperate, but more than that, I do not want two kinds of people involved in youth work:

1. Those who respond to the open invite for the wrong reasons, often guilt induced, with no sense of call.
2. Those who I think would be a danger to young people (I admit, often based on a subjective hunch), and it is hard on an interpersonal level to say no to someone when you have effectively put a plea out there.

I do not want warm bodies involved in youth work, people there to make up the numbers. Consider making it policy that people do not ask for volunteers from the front. The hand-on-shoulder approach is crucially initiated by you, having spent time prayerfully considering who might be the best fit in terms of the 5 Cs discussed in the next chapter, and I would suggest, will bear more fruit and cause less problems down the line. This approach roots itself in relationship. I volunteered at a church that do not allow people to take up positions of leadership for a minimum of 6 months on joining, to allow people to get to know each other first. Better to scale

---

22. Saunders, *Youth Work From Scratch*, 39-40.

down your operation than have a team full of people who are there to make up numbers.

PRINCIPLE NUMBER THREE: UPGRADE BEFORE YOU ARRIVE

I am a Mac convert. Not only does my workplace swear by Apple products, but I have seen the benefits. Since making the move, similar to switching blue shirt for red on Merseyside, or Red Sox to Yankees for those Stateside, I have not looked back. Gone are the virus-infested, motherboard-wrestling days as a PC owner. I calculated that I have spent about a week of my life installing and re-installing variants of a certain operating system. A frustrating experience was getting hold of the latest game, getting home, and finding that the machine did not have the resources to quite deliver the goods, even on the lowest game settings. At least with a frame rate of one per second you had time to avoid the enemy. This experience would lead me to a choice: upgrade or return the game. I learned the hard way that the time to upgrade was when the games were playing flawlessly.

Continuing the theme, founder of tech-giant IBM, Tom Watson, said that the company enjoyed the success that it had for three reasons:

1. "At the very beginning I had a very clear picture of what the company would look like when it was finally done.
2. Once I had that picture I then asked myself how a company that looked like that would have to act.
3. Once I had a picture in place [. . .] and how such a company would have to act, I then realized that unless we began to act that way from the very beginning we would never get there. In other words, [. . .] it would have to act like a great company long before it ever became one."[23]

If you have all the vision in the world, but cannot translate it into definable actions, you will do little more than daydream. Thinking that you will achieve your vision one person at a time is noble and touching, but what happens when teenagers show up *en-masse*? Watson calls us to act the next level up, to upgrade before it is needed. If you want the results you are

---

23. Watson, quoted in Gerber, *The E-Myth Revisited*.

getting, keep doing what you are doing—you have the perfect strategy. If you want to grow, change before you need to.

One of the most useful models for helping me understand starting, restarting and revitalising youth work in light of this is the S-Curve based on the sigmoid function in math, or at least, its application to organisations, which is how Charles Handy interpreted it[24] although it is also used in areas such as pharmacology and agriculture! While the mathematical function is now a distant memory, essentially the model captures three phases: Learning, Growing and Declining, as shown in Figure 8.

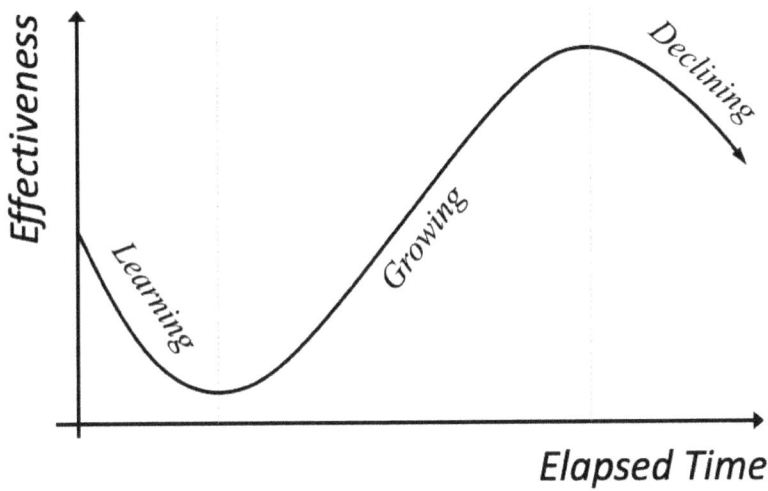

Figure 8: The S-Curve

This appears almost universal, reflecting our human life cycle as much as the latest Mac product. Phase 1 tells me that it is OK when I have started a youth work when, despite hours of investment at schools raising awareness, just three teens turn up to your event. Do not give up! In theological terms, this is often called dying to self. Your hopes and aspirations (as well as the financial resources of others!) seem on the line. John 12:24 illustrates this with a farming analogy: "Unless a grain of wheat falls to the ground and dies, it remains a single seed. But if it dies, it produces many seeds." In business-speak, if you do not speculate, you do not accumulate, and this is the time when you are building trust with young people, and trust is a

---

24. Handy, "Where are you" *Directors and Boards*.

fragile commodity in the early days. But see this through, and the power of buy-in begins to deliver.[25] In Phase 2 you get to sample the sweet taste of success, riding the wave of effectiveness, with the youth project bursting at the seams and people throwing money at you as they see the outcomes rolling out. Eventually, however, decline occurs. Phase 3 creeps up on you, sneaking in when you are still living the high life. Soon, your product looks antiquated (consider how we talk about "bricks"—mobile phones that once were the must-have product) and the interest isn't there no matter how good your promotion. I have experienced that with a youth drop-in that we continued long past its sell-by date, still seeing several teens accessing it each week, but far from its heyday.

Renewal is difficult in decline, and resurrection is a divine task; consider the fate of high street names such as *ToysRUs* and *Blockbuster*. Companies such as these are often bought by investors who are not interested in reviving the business, but in breaking it up to sell the core components, such as distribution networks and properties. However, your start up does not need to end in decline and death. There is life beyond the curve. "The secret to constant growth is to start [. . .] that second curve at a point where there is time, as well as the resources and energy, to get the new curve through its initial explorations and floundering before the first curve begins to dip downwards."[26] Figure 9 shows the best time to bring change, with the dotted line indicating what could happen if you do nothing: There are denominations right now throwing phenomenal amounts of resources at new, fresh initiatives, because they have found themselves staring down the barrel in the declining stage. It's virtually too late for them. The main line denominations haemorrhaged young people in the 80s and 90s, with investment now decades too late. Some churches seem to have accepted their fate, and now simply consolidate and die, albeit rather slowly. I read the public minutes of a denomination's annual meeting which recorded 39 churches closing their doors for the last time between March 2014 and April 2016, with no new expressions of church in that time. The minutes noted the closures, "with praise to God for the worship and witness offered by these fellowships across the years."[27] I'm sorry, but shouldn't that read, "notes the closures with anger and disappointment that the gospel

---

25. Maxwell, *The 21 Irrefutable Laws*, Ch14.

26. Handy, *The Age of Paradox*, 51.

27. See http://urc.org.uk/images/General-Assemblies/Assembly2016/assembly_reports_16.pdf 47.

had ceased to bear fruit in those fellowships, and establish a fierce resolve to establish a work of prayer and mission to take back the ground lost"?

Life between the curves . . . is scary. There is confusion, and even real loss before the growth occurs. Think of what life was like post-Pentecost. The question facing the early followers of Jesus was the nature of the new faith. Was it still Judaism? To what extent was the law applicable to both Jewish and Gentile believers? We have the narrative and two thousand years of church history, but those early men and women were stepping into the unknown. Consider Peter's own journey, confronted over his own myopic views of who was "in" or "out"—clean or unclean—through a divine vision (Acts 10). Without these difficult and complex moments the faith would not have gone worldwide.

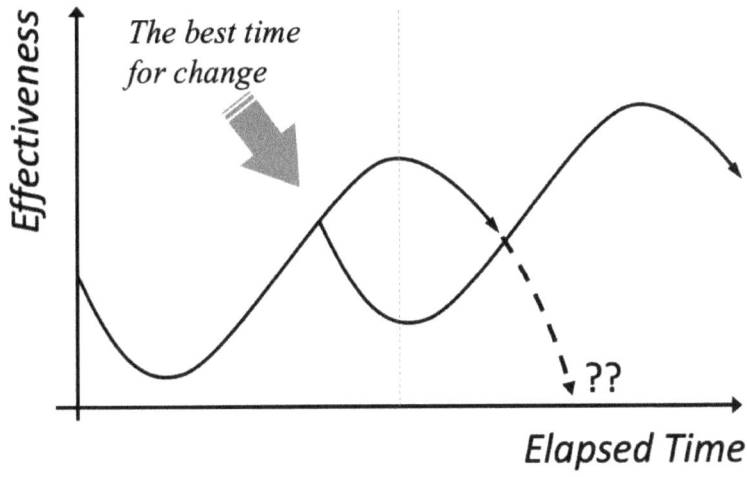

Figure 9: Hacking the S-Curve

Multiple curves allow for different seasons of a church or organisation's life. In the early days, there is the energy and excitement of doing something new and breaking new ground. This period is often high on relationship and flexibility, networking to find the best way forward. Yet at some stage entrepreneurial start-ups need structural upgrades; cue the new curve, experienced as destroying spontaneity, sapping energy and becoming bureaucratic. Morris summarizes that "scholars dispute what level of institutionalization is revealed within the body of Christ texts"[28] and Luke, the

---

28. Morris, *Flexible Church*, 108.

author of the book of Acts, seems to have little or no interest in church organisation or polity,"[29] perhaps reflecting the more organic way Paul was operating. Yet what the metaphor does provide is a flexible structure that can adapt to the changing contexts that the body finds itself in: from the underground church in North Korea to Nashville, TN, considered by many to be the buckle of the Bible belt. Underground churches may not be so forever, and the shift in culture is unmistakable even in the most churched of states in America's deep south. Bruggemann contends that this is permissible, stating that, 'models of the church must not be dictated by cultural reality, but they must be voiced and practiced in ways that take careful account of the particular time and circumstance into which God's people are called. Every model of the church must be critically contextual.'[30] Welcoming new seasons will cost, but this isn't change for change's sake; this is ensuring that what you start outlasts you. That must be the end game for every youth worker. Change fatigue occurs when you start afresh before you get to enjoy real success—a premature second curve. Done right and finishing well will not be so much of an end as a new beginning.

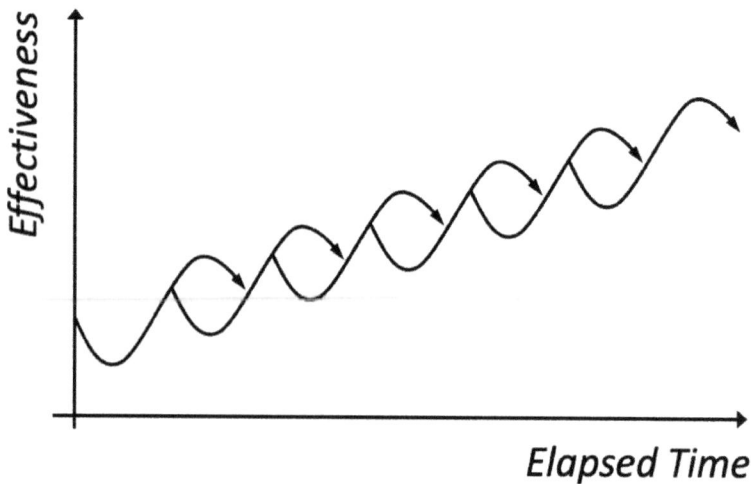

Figure 10: Riding the S-Wave

---

29. Fee and Stuart, *How to Read the Bible*, 112.
30. Brueggemann, "Rethinking Church Models," 129.

FOR REFLECTION AND DISCUSSION:

1. In what areas are you looking for prefabbed success?
2. To what extent are you enjoying the *process* of youth work and ministry, or are you enduring things to get to the goal?
3. What would it look like to go to the next level in your youth work and ministry? How can you get there?

CHAPTER ACTION POINTS:

Stakeholders

1. Make a list of those you could consider *stakeholders*.
2. Are the relationships with each clearly understood by both parties?
3. Under each one, note what you have done, are doing and could do to nurture the relationships.

Partnerships

1. Map your locality, identifying those groups, bodies and individuals that you partner with.
2. Describe the relationship. Put a plus sign by those you want to develop, and a minus sign by those you want to lessen, and consider the implications of that action.
3. Who is conspicuous by their absence? Go over the map a second time and, using a search engine and local knowledge, add in the location and profile of other youth work providers.
4. Follow up on each, even if it simply means popping your head around the door to acknowledge their existence!

5

Airbrushed youth ministry

How to put together a theologically rich dream team

IN THIS CHAPTER, I encourage us not to accept low standards. Yet how can we really be picky in youth work when working with volunteers who give up their precious nights to be sworn at, ignored, pushed to their human limits and frustrated? What if you *are* that volunteer? Keep reading . . .

CAN YOU AFFORD NOT TO BE PICKY?

For those in the majority of UK church settings the American staff team seems like a mirage in the desert. You need to be about *Building a Kingdom Dream Team*, so look for those with character, competence and chemistry, look from within before you throw the net wider, and do not settle for second best.[1] But many of us do not have that luxury. How can we afford to be picky when we are short of volunteers for Thursday's additional needs group, Friday night's open access club, the detached team on Saturday, or the Sunday morning ministry?

I think the more important question is how can you afford not to be picky?

Simply put, within a church setting, some members are a danger to young people. I do not want superheroes working with young people. Someone will eventually tip Bruce Banner over the edge. It doesn't end well. *Onesies* were part and parcel of popular youth culture in 2018-19,

---

1. Hybels, *Courageous Leadership*, 73-92.

but Catwoman is straight up inappropriate. I'm also concerned about Peter Parker's inconsistency, always promising to be there, yet often conspicuous by his absence. There's nothing quite like letting young people down. Tony Stark's entrepreneurial skills would be fantastic, if he can leave his ego at the door and bring Pepper Potts with him to act as an interpreter and emotional buffer. Bruce Wayne is socially inept, and downright moody with the cape on, and Clark Kent's X-Ray vision poses serious safeguarding concerns.

Can you imagine the risk assessments needed with this lot?

Part of the role of the youth worker is to pastor young people, whether you have the word in your title or not. The word, *pastor*, comes from the Latin for *shepherd* and, in the Old Testament, the shepherd protected the sheep from hungry predators and equally determined thieves, even if it meant risking personal safety to ensure theirs. This marked out the shepherd from the *hired hand*, who would abandon the poor sheep when under attack (John 10:13). They may have been alone, but that did not mean defenseless: They were armed. The shepherd's crook was not his only weapon; slung round his neck was a rod, a *shevet* in Hebrew. This intimidating wooden club was designed to tell the raider in no uncertain terms not to come back in a hurry.

There have been several occasions where I could have done with a *shevet*, as my first concern is the welfare and well-being of the young people. There have been times when I have refused someone permission to be involved in youth work, and yet I had no reason other than an uncomfortable feeling. One woman had what seemed to be legitimate concerns over our safeguarding policy, but when she dragged her feet over the Criminal Records check (now DBS in the UK) we stopped the process, led by my concern for the young people. Churches are complicated, as many adults do have access to young people that you have little say about. It would be a logistical nightmare to ensure every church attendee was subjected to a background check, but safeguarding policy demands should be non-negotiable and part of the shepherding role.

While the vast majority of the references to shepherd in the New Testament are related to Jesus, there are a handful that point towards Christian workers.

Paul recognized the calling of some to be shepherds (ESV—rendered *pastors* in the NIV) in Ephesians 4:11, and instructs the elders in Ephesus to "keep watch over yourselves and all the flock of which the Holy Spirit has made you overseers. Be shepherds of the church of God, which He bought with His own blood" (Acts 20:28).

Peter was perhaps more profoundly impacted by the imagery, as his reinstatement by Jesus was centered on the instruction to literally "shepherd My sheep" in the second response from Jesus in John 21:16. This theme continues into Peter's letters, with elders called to "shepherd the flock of God among you" in 1 Peter 5:1-2.

COMPLEMENTING CHARACTERISTICS

The Old Testament knew shepherding. In the back end of Genesis, Pharaoh was happy to accommodate Jacob and sons, with the family business in sheep rearing going back generations (Genesis 47:3). However, he restricted them to Goshen, in part because that's where the pasture land was, but also because shepherds were considered *"detestable to the Egyptians"* (Genesis 46:34), and this area was at arms-length from the main cities. Later on, in the words of Psalm 78:70-72:

> "[God] chose David his servant
> and took him from the sheep pens;
> from tending the sheep he brought him
> to be the shepherd of his people Jacob,
> of Israel his inheritance.
> And David shepherded them with integrity of heart;
> with skilful hands he led them."

Without doubt, David was the closest thing in the Old Testament to an "all-singing" (he penned 50% of the Psalms), "all-dancing" (who can forget his breakdancing in 2 Samuel 6:14), "omni-competent" leader (the little guy beat the big guy in 1 Samuel 17).[2] Yet who can forget the pivotal story of his later leadership—the sexual scandal involving Bathsheba. Despite clear repentance (Psalm 51), David's leadership took a hit, and he never seems to fully recover. A deeper reading of the text reveals a detail that is often missed by biographers: just who he put to death to cover up the unwanted pregnancy. Bathsheba's husband was hand-picked by David himself, and was counted amongst the Thirty (see Appendix 2). These *mighty men* would gladly have died for their shepherd-king and were drawn from the 400 men

---

2. Pilavachi, "The Vision: The Youth Worker," 24.

who gathered around David while in exile (1 Samuel 22:1-2). The irony is that David's own downfall was surrounding himself with men of integrity, as he couldn't manipulate them with flattery or rewards. In Uriah, he chose someone better than himself. That's leadership. The story contrasts with Jephthah in Judges 11:3 who, like David, fled his family to exile, yet soon "had a band of worthless rebels following him." The Old Testament does not typically speak kindly about leadership.

The fact that the New Testament speaks so little about Christian workers as shepherds means that the analogy must not be over stretched. Bryn Hughes contends that, "the overwhelming weight of evidence is that the pattern of caring within the church should be based on the principle of "one anothering" [of which] there are 57 references."[3] Shepherding is best seen as a function of leadership, and the solitary shepherd is a model of leadership we must avoid: they were the Old Testament club-swinging, lion-taming, insomniac Avengers. The youth worker is to use their leadership to release others into leadership roles and act as a gatekeeper. Andy Stanley is brutal:

> "[It's the first-century word. If Jesus were here today, would he talk about shepherds? No. He would point to something that we all know, and we'd say, "Oh yeah, I know what that is." Jesus told Peter, the fisherman, to "feed my sheep," but he didn't say to the rest of them, "Go ye therefore into all the world and be shepherds and feed my sheep." By the time of the Book of Acts, the shepherd model is gone. It's about establishing elders and deacons and their qualifications.[4]

Returning then to the characteristics for building the team, Hybels suggests *Character, Competence* and *Chemistry*. In 2010 he added a fourth, *Culture*.[5] I contend that we should also be looking for *Calling*, and I would advocate this 5-fold approach to building your dream team.

1. Character

    One of the joys of youth work is when you see a young person step up to a challenge. Dan had been part of a group of lads who had seriously offended two girls. I challenged him over this and, despite

---

3. Hughes, *Small Group Know How*, 34-35.
4. Stanley, "Get it done," 28.
5. Hybels, *Willow Creek Summit 2010*, http://www.willowcreekglobalsummit.com/downloads/here_to_there/fantastic_people/Here_to_There_-_Fantastic_People_Outline_and_Process_Tool.pdf (accessed 22.3.13).

an initial sense of unfairness that it wasn't entirely his fault, he took responsibility and apologized sincerely, making appropriate amends. Above all of the other traits, we value character. We want to be able to trust those we work with, as Kouzes & Posner suggest, "the ultimate test of leaders' credibility is whether they do as they say."[6] Character, integrity and credibility are all hard-won . . . and easily lost. They do not preclude mistakes but ensure that they are owned and that the blame is not passed on. When I have been falsely accused, character has demanded that I do not retaliate. When I am tempted to take a short cut behind the scenes, character demands that I act consistently with my public presence. As a Christian, I recognize that I cannot do anything when no one is looking, as I believe in a God who is always present (Psalm 139:1-18). Character is living continually for the audience of One, whether I am alone in my room, or on stage in front of thousands. This is first in priority for good reason. When the apostles looked to resolve a problem with the daily distribution of food in Acts 6, they delegated authority to the body of disciples to select seven people, setting two criteria, which had nothing to do with administrative ability or efficiency: That they be "full of the Spirit and wisdom." These are hard to measure but easy to see, and are about who the person is, not what they can do.

2. Competence

Every part of the body has a job to do, and if the body is to function effectively, each part must be competent. Following a leg injury, I lay on my front at the sports physio, and was told that, for all of my effort, I was exerting just a fraction of the force I should be capable of. My muscles had lost capacity to do the job. The good news is that competence is the easiest of the five areas to develop, with a range of training options and tools available, but there are some bottom line skills that will be dictated by the role you wish to fill. Many job adverts want someone with a *proven* track record. Graduates learn to hate those words. With volunteers and young leaders, I am generally more than ready to give them a chance with no record behind them if other characteristics are satisfied, as coaching can make a difference in a short space of time. However, some situations call for proof of competence, and a list of experiences contributes little, as this measures quantity, not quality.

6. Kouzes, and Posner, *Credibility*, 185.

3. Chemistry

Hybels speaks of looking for "a relational fit with me as well as with other team members"[7] and this is best assessed through simply hanging out with each other. If you are interviewing someone for a role on the team, schedule some down time, involve food and aim for informality. This is a great way to see if you will gel. I was shortlisted for a youth pastor job at a mega church in New Jersey and the pastor asked me to listen to a few of his sermons online. Why? His ego? Not at all. It was because he wanted people on his team who could sit under his teaching, and root for him. I understand that, and have seen that when early cracks are ignored, they can become huge chasms that cannot be crossed later on. I love the creative spark and synergy that exists when team workers love spending time with each other. When I worked at a traditional, older church, I had to ask myself, "would I attend if I wasn't being paid to?" That was challenging, but one that I could answer in the affirmative, with a number of people that I would want with me on any leadership team.

4. Culture

Since the 1990's there has been an increased focus on articulating the values that churches and organisations hold. These values shape culture, and those you work with need to be able to buy in to these. When I was the pastor of a church in Oxfordshire, I saw Sunday morning as a shop window and recognized that, as a dormitory village lying within a commuter belt for London, there were implications for the church. I made sure that services started on time, to reduce the barriers for professionals to attend the church service. This *culture* bled into much of the youth work we did and set expectations. Moving to Bournemouth, we joined a young church and became volunteers in their youth work. Suffice to say that punctuality was not a core value! While I joked with the pastor, I quickly bought into the values of the church. They are not wrong to be casual about time; in fact, this can demonstrate a commitment to people over tasks. It is simply different. It is crucial that team members buy in to the cultural values. This reduces complaints, breeds consistency, yet allows for creativity.

---

7. Hybels, *Courageous Leadership*, 84.

5. Calling

Finally, is there a sense of calling to be part of what is going on? Os Guiness writes, "A sense of call should precede a choice of job and career. [. . .] Instead of, 'you are what you do', calling says: 'Do what you are.'"[8] I am looking for that passion to be present in the team around me. Whether it is being employed or getting involved as a volunteer oftentimes there are circumstances and events that act as affirmations that God is in it, and logging these in some manner, whether committing to memory or writing in a journal, is important. The affirmation and evidential signs are useful in a number of ways. Firstly, they confirm the rightness of where you are going and what you are doing. Secondly, they are evidence for those around you that this is the right thing. I want to know that those around me feel called to be involved, because call goes far beyond contract. Finally, when everything else is out at sea and life has whipped up a tempest that makes you doubt whether you should still be involved, a sense of call is the anchor in the storm.

There are tensions. While I want to be surrounded by people I "click" with, I also value those who challenge my way of thinking, as long as I can trust where they are coming from. I had great respect for a deacon who was a stickler for detail, although this was not so from the start. Initially, the fine toothcomb that he applied to my ideas was frustrating, until I realized that he was bringing particular skills to the table that I did not possess.

These characteristics should shape our teams, and we should be unapologetic: "Keep the selection bar high."[9] The critical issue is that my insecurities do not prevent people better than me being on the team. If they tick the boxes above, it should give a clear indication that they will make a great contribution. You might even assess those currently involved against the criteria, using the following matrix in figure 11 to help if someone scores a 4 out of 5.

---

8. Guiness, *The Call*, 46.
9. Hybels, *Courageous Leadership*, 85.

Criteria	How to discern in interview	If not present in interview stage	Next step for potential member	Next step for existing member
Character	Probing questions. Contact with previous colleagues.	Stop process. This needs resolving, but your team is not the place.	Recommend a discipleship year, and Christian disciplines.	Step back from face-to-face youth work. Assign mentor.
Competence	Lead a youth activity or group. Present to panel.	Continue if a gap in skills exists, or there is a sense of potential.	Training—can be offered in house, or look for courses.	Training—can be offered in house, or look for courses.
Chemistry	Relational activity with team. Time with individuals, especially line manager. Possible psychometric tests.	Slow process down.	Create opportunities for relationship building.	Consider team building activities, and training such as Belbin's interlocking team roles (see Ch6)
Culture	Questions about previous roles and values. Investigate previous employment.	Proceed with caution.	Exposure to wider ministries before making decision.	Teaching on church / ministry values. Assign mentor from leadership team.
Calling	Questions about why this is the right role for them. Evidence that this is more than a career move.	Stop process.	They need to reflect on where they are going.	Create space for reflection, e.g., team retreat. If needed give a sabbatical.

Figure 11: Employment Selection Matrix

It is always better to forsake employment than bring the wrong person on board, and calling time on a project is better than running something with square pegs in round holes.

SIGNING UP FOR MORE THAN YOU BARGAINED FOR

I was a mid-season signing, having recently joined the church. Following #thehandshake with the youth pastor (see the Instagram post in figure 12) I donned the subtly-logoed T-shirt and met the rest of the team for a pep talk and prayer before the young people arrived.

Figure 12: #thehandshake

It was clear that they knew each other well, with some who were recent graduates of the youth ministry. Being extroverted, and having served in other churches in similar capacities, it was relatively easy to build relationships and get involved. It is amazing how your personality counts in youth work. My hope would be that had I presented as more reticent, or had it not been obvious that I am extroverted, the youth pastor would have appropriately welcomed me, perhaps buddying me up with a more experienced hand, and taken some of the pressure off. Len Kageler, former professor at Nyack College, NY, observes that, "although they are not listed along with the gifts of the Spirit, personality differences are described throughout the Bible."[10] We read of Saul in 1 Samuel 10, who despite his impressive physique, actually hid behind luggage to avoid the clamor for his presence! And who can miss the "foot-in-mouth", impulsive and extroverted nature of Peter? The danger in youth ministry is that only extroverts are prized, yet a team that has no introverts will scare some young people away, and a lack of reflective types will never stop long enough to identify what has been going well and what hasn't. They will miss some of the details.

Don't be afraid to say what you are and are not comfortable doing. Leaders and managers want you to come back again and again, not under duress but because you feel valued, if not by young people then by the team, and that your contribution makes a difference. My wife, and long-term partner in youth work and ministry, is a little more introverted than I am. She doesn't want to stand up and lead activities, and is happiest facilitating youth work in the background, ensuring forms are completed, and registering young people in at the door when doing open access work. This has the additional benefit of helping her get to know the names of young people, rather than the catchall, *"hey buddy!"* approach. She is also great at building deep relationships with a few young people that will last beyond the teenage years, evidenced by the number of *ex-youth* who stay in touch or come and visit.

And you are likewise uniquely gifted and experienced to connect with young people that others can't. Ann was one of my all-time favorite "extra-timers." Being polite (and crucially not being involved in the safeguarding process), I never discovered her age, but she was several generations removed from the young people. She didn't know the language, care for the music, or abide by the non-smart dress policy, but she loved young people, and they knew it. More often than not, Ann would be seen sitting next to a young person, listening intently to their every word, not worried if the activities had moved on, or the room had otherwise vacated. Ann didn't have the title, and wouldn't have wanted it, but she was a pastor to many of the teens and related in a way that I just couldn't.

Me? Let me take you back to #thehandshake. Within five minutes, I'm in with the guys playing indoor soccer (it was literally only boys for 2.5 out of 3 hours), and by the end of night one, I am literally dripping with sweat. I also have procured a set of six or seven names that I have repeated

10. Kageler, *The Volunteer's Field Guide*, 17.

as often as I could through the evening without sounding weird so that I could remember them, and looked to pass young people in, rather than showboat my skills. I've had to learn that one in youth ministry! But this has all been at the expense of connecting more broadly, moving room to room. We make choices, and that's OK. But after three weeks, it feels a bit awkward. New volunteers need those who have been around a little longer to reassure them, make non-cringy introductions to young people, and fill in the gaps in knowledge that will exist.

I touched base with the youth pastor outside of the youth nights, and it was evident that the relationship was strong enough to ask questions about what he was trying to do, and how I could fit in with that vision. I've also done this before—I know what to do as a volunteer. You may not. Scheduling time with the head-honcho outside of the pressured youth work environment is essential, and here are some questions you may wish to ask:

- Is there a role description? If not, what exactly do you want me to do?
- What happens when things go wrong?
- Are there rules, or a code of conduct that young people have signed up to?
- What kind of behavior do you tolerate/not tolerate?
- What's the commitment you expect?
- How do I know if I'm doing a good job?
- What training do you provide?

You can text or email this list if opening it up in conversation feels awkward or too forceful. This time round however, as I began to get involved, I hit unexpected issues—and gained an invaluable insight into the extra-timers. Aside from a few minor things, my young children took turns to visit the hospital, and I had two big, unforeseen projects land on me at work that impacted how early I could get out on a Friday, and to the youth work. As much as I wanted to be there, circumstance prevented me. The only saving grace was the team was sufficiently big to not be impacted by my absence. I realized that many do youth work whilst maintaining unpredictable family, work and social dynamics.

If you are that youth pastor or manager, take the initiative to draw up role descriptions and listen to the demands on your volunteer team. Encourage them in their gifting and remind them of the part they play and the difference they make. As volunteers who do not necessarily carry the administrative and management responsibilities, they are able to serve the body as the hands and feet, as close to the action as it gets. They are the parts of the body that deserve more honor.

WHY I AM NOT A VOLUNTEER (EVEN IF YOU PRINT IT ON MY T-SHIRT)

Put me in any church and I don't need a desperate plea from the front, my arm twisted behind my back, or incentives that I "only need commit to once a month." I will be involved in some way. Here's the thing:

I'm not first and foremost a volunteer.

I don't see myself in that way, there to make up the numbers, or help with the trip. I am a disciple of Christ, part of His body, and I want to both grow as a disciple and contribute to the growth of others. If I sit on the sidelines, I deprive the body of Christ of the unique contribution I can make, and bad things happen. Ever sat on a chair too long? Your legs go to sleep, or worse, develop pins and needles. We weren't designed to sit down all day, although this is the reality for many. Our legs were designed for walking, running, and jumping—my two-year-old can attest to that. And you were set apart, uniquely gifted to serve and contribute to the body of Christ.

This is not semantics, a clever word play, but connects serving as part of the body of Christ with being a disciple. This becomes our primary disposition. In Figure 13 I contrast the notion of the volunteers with the disciple:

A volunteer...	A disciple	Scripture
has rights.	recognises their life is not their own, but that they were *"bought at a price."*	1 Corinthians 6:20
should have high expectations of treatment.	anticipates troubles and hardship.	John 16:33
can step down at any time.	serves relentlessly to the end.	Luke 9:23, 14:33
shouldn't be expected of.	has got a field to harvest, and is expected to provide a return on investment.	Matthew 9:35-38, Matthew 25:14-30
should enjoy being involved.	derives joy from sacrificial service.	Philippians 2:17

A volunteer...	A disciple	Scripture
should expect to be rewarded.	knows their reward is in heaven.	Matthew 16:27, Philippians 3:14
responds to request for help.	initiates their involvement.	Matthew 8:15, Luke 19:10

Figure 13: Volunteer Vs Disciple

This in no way softens the standard of care and investment for those who serve young people from a manager, youth pastor or leader, but suggests that we view our involvement personally through the lens of discipleship, rather than of volunteerism.

I don't want to leave on a potentially false dichotomy. The church is not a voluntary organisation, but a living organism that understands the symbiotic relationship between the individual parts. You might choose to use the term *volunteer*. That's fine! In fact, extra-timers can be actively discipled through their engagement as volunteers. Ephesians 4:12 identifies leadership roles "to equip his people for works of service, so that the body of Christ may be built up." Leaders should aim to deliver the highest standard of care and investment for their volunteers, yet personally model what disciples should look like. Leaders have the privilege and challenge of shaping the body, although the blueprints have already been provided by the author, pioneer and perfecter of the faith, Jesus Christ (Hebrews 12:2).

FOR REFLECTION AND DISCUSSION:

1. If you have any management role, what characteristics do you look for in those you bring in? Can you list the 5 Cs in order of importance?
2. What would you say the organisation or church looks for, and values?
3. Thinking beyond your own setting, who would you LOVE to work with in youth work / ministry? It can be anyone! Who makes your dream team? Why? What would they add that you don't currently have?

4. Looking at figure 13, to what extent do you see yourself as a disciple rather than as a volunteer?

CHAPTER ACTION POINTS:

1. Set up a meeting with your line manager / youth worker / pastor and follow up on the list of questions below figure 12.

6

Beyond the nip and tuck
How to develop a healthy body image

WHILE MANY IN THE Christian world missed it, a new bible was released in 2007 that instantly gained UK best-seller status. Trinny and Susannah's *The Body Shape Bible* created a body shape typology,[1] and based on this, the two women were able to make generic judgement calls on what clothes would both flatter and suit the person in front of them. This was launched in the surf created by Gok Wan's *How to Look Good Naked*, aired in the UK first in 2006 by Channel 4, which helped people who were insecure about their body image to get out on the catwalk, having first worked on self-esteem issues by literally projecting a woman's curves onto the side of a building.[2] Since then we have had a slew of cheap programming focussed on outward presentation. A friend was involved with the show and spoke highly of Gok when off screen, being a quiet, thoughtful individual. But one example from a shoot stuck with her: Gok was in full flow, when a sharp voice ground the proceedings to a halt.

"Did you really mean to use that word? I'm not sure it conveys the message you want it to . . . "

They re-shot the "unscripted" scene, this time without the offending word. Image is everything. To "The Fairy Gok Mother's" credit, the show steered away from tummy tucks, boob augmentation and liposuction, yet its success only magnifies our obsession with image which permeates

1. Woodall and Constantine, *The Body Shape Bible*.
2. Well, that's just one example of what Gok's team did!

everything, from what fills our wardrobes to how we construct our church programmes, dress up our services and express our faith publicly.

It's easy to fall into the trap of style over substance. Question: Have you ever played basketball with Jesus? During the summer of 1997 I played basketball on the streets of Camden, NJ, with Jesus (pronounced Hey-Zeus), and Travis. Jesus was good, but Travis was phenomenally gifted. He single-handedly destroyed the first two teams we played with some sublime skill. Inevitably we faced a decent outfit in the semis. After what seemed like hours of working the asphalt and getting nowhere, I called a timeout. Travis had gone solo, trying complex layups and shots that were just not working out, and the rest of the team were beginning to marginalize him. I challenged his attitude, and to look to pass when on the offensive rather than take on their entire team.

Travis: "Coach, I want people to remember my name. I'd rather lose looking good."

Fortunately, the rest of the team disagreed, and we scraped that win with some ugly ball, and went on to take the championship.

Perhaps it isn't just style. Maybe it is statistics over substance. If churches and youth programmes record anything, it is the following two pieces of data: attendance and finance. I would advocate ensuring you are tracking these two figures, but whilst important, they skew the perspective about growth towards the superficial, and can mask the critical issue of spiritual growth. You can have over one hundred attendees and not one disciple—slick, well-resourced youth ministry that draws a crowd and not one young person who graduates to regular church attendance.

So what are the vital signs of health in our churches?

I led the youth team of a church in a large town, and after two years all of us felt that we needed to close the ministry down. That wasn't a typo. Independent of each other, we had come to conclude that the church did not own the youth work, and it was being staffed by college students on placement, and one recent graduate (me). We presented this to the elders ... who disagreed. Over the next year we had all moved on, and the youth ministry slowly ground to a halt. A healthy church owns the youth ministry, integrating it into the main body of activity and life. College students on placement should be the cherry on the top, and an opportunity to invest in them, rather than the main ingredient doing the job for the church that others are not willing to do. Creasy Dean pitches in, that "Youth ministry is the church's ministry, not just that of specialists who can "relate" to the young people."[3]

It's vital we have a healthy body image in the church, but also within youth work itself. Sam and Jess wrapped up the youth-led service in prayer and looked across at me for some clues as what to do next. I swept across the stage and took the mic. "Let's hear it for our young people!" Cue the applause, sustained for over 60 seconds. Awkward smiles all round. I clap Sam on his back and punch Jess' shoulder (obviously the type that doesn't leave a mark, except to say, "Proud of you! You were awesome!) and begin to make my way to thank the techies at the back. Jess' mum and gran block my path and thank me "for all you've done with Jess and the rest of the youths" (youths! I hate that expression!) I smile, and look to move past, when gran chips in,

"We could do with 15 of you!"

I moved on, but something in me had jarred, and wouldn't let the comment go. No we couldn't! Two of me, let alone 15, would be a complete, unmitigated disaster! I knew it intuitively, but why?

WINNING TEAMS AREN'T HEAD AND SHOULDERS ABOVE THE REST

Meredith Belbin's seminal research on management teams proves without a doubt that teams require different types of people and roles in order to be successful. Like many of us, he asked, "Why not create a team entirely composed of clever people, amply endowed for coping with major projects and big decisions?"[4] His investigation was damning: They "seemed to have a flair for spotting the weak points of the other's argument. There was [. . .] no coherence in the decisions that the team reached—or was forced to reach—and several pressing and necessary jobs were totally neglected."[5] Hughes summarizes Belbin's roles as follows in Figure 14, noting that few of us are capable in more than two of them:

---

3. Creasy Dean, quoted in Devries, *Sustainable Youth Ministry*, 142.
4. Belbin, *Management Teams*, 13.
5. Belbin, *Management Teams*, 14.

Title of Style	Function	Positive Characteristics	Permissible Weaknesses
Plant	Source of original ideas	Creative, unorthodox, imaginative	Impractical, unrealistic
Monitor evaluator	Accurate judgement	Pragmatic, detached, clear thinking	Cold, clinical, critical, uninspiring
Resource investigator	Knows the team's context, brings fresh information	Wide outside contacts, extrovert, inquisitive	Does not sustain interest, little task focus
Completer finisher	Finishes the job Dots 'i's and crosses 't's	Attention to detail, thorough, precise	Low people skills, perfectionist nitpicking in details
Company worker	Strategic planning	Practical. Diligent Administrative skills Structured thinker	Inflexible, conservative
Teamworker	Oils the wheels Listens and interprets Brings harmony	Relational, sensitive, accepting	Avoids confrontation Indecisive Low emphasis on results
Chairperson	Integrates the individual contributions Holds the process to the agenda	Accepting of diverse contributions Clear sense of purpose and direction	Not necessarily creative or academic
Shaper	Challenges the mediocre and the slow Strives for the best	Dynamic, lots of drive, passionate	Tetchy, irritable, intolerant

Figure 14: Belbin's Team Roles[6]

Belbin makes three points regarding winning teams:

- "Winning companies possessed good Team Role balance.
- Compensating for lack of balance can have a favorable effect on a team's prospects.

---

6. Hughes, *Leadership Toolkit*, 188.

- Awareness of Team Roles helps to improve companies' performance."[7]

But this is nothing new. The apostle Paul articulated team management long before Belbin, using a model that we affirm from the front-stage but deny through our behavior behind the curtains and off-stage decisions: The body of Christ in 1 Corinthians 12, that Dunn refers to as "the dominant theological image in Pauline ecclesiology."[8] This concept renders a team full of shepherds crooked, and reminds us that even the "genius, billionaire, playboy, philanthropist" Tony Stark needs a Pepper Potts.[9]

> 7 Now to each one the manifestation of the Spirit is given for the common good. [. . .] 12 Just as a body, though one, has many parts, but all its many parts form one body, so it is with Christ. For we were all baptized by one Spirit so as to form one body [. . .] and we were all given the one Spirit to drink. 14 Even so the body is not made up of one part but of many.
>
> 18 . . . in fact God has placed the parts in the body, every one of them, just as he wanted them to be. 19 If they were all one part, where would the body be? 20 As it is, there are many parts, but one body.
>
> 21 The eye cannot say to the hand, "I don't need you!" And the head cannot say to the feet, "I don't need you!" 22 On the contrary, those parts of the body that seem to be weaker are indispensable, 23 and the parts that we think are less honorable we treat with special honor. And the parts that are unpresentable are treated with special modesty, 24 while our presentable parts need no special treatment. But God has put the body together, giving greater honor to the parts that lacked it, 25 so that there should be no division in the body, but that its parts should have equal concern for each other.26 If one part suffers, every part suffers with it; if one part is honored, every part rejoices with it.
>
> 27 Now you are the body of Christ, and each one of you is a part of it. (NIV)

Morris sets the scene well, noting that

> "Paul introduced the metaphor to those whose faith was being distorted by the culture of first century Corinth, which [. . .] resonates with contemporary Western culture as regards the West's: consumerist culture; 'postmodern' ethos; emphasis on social

---

7. Belbin, *Management Teams*, 107.
8. Dunn, *The Theology of Paul*, 548.
9. Whedon, *The Avengers*.

Beyond the Nip and Tuck

construction; preoccupation with individual autonomy; pursuit of success; elevation of substance less audience-pleasing rhetoric; and a desire for relativistic 'local' theology."[10]

From this, and the complementary passages in Ephesians 4, Romans 12 and Colossians 1 and 2 we have an alternative to the superhero construct: Every member ministry.

One body, church or team, but many parts, with the grand total more than the sum of the parts. As Fee writes, this "does not mean uniformity [. . .] Paul's concern is for their unity; but there is no such unity without diversity."[11] However, this too often receives lip service, as we act out of our own insecurities, and what goes on in the head is replicated throughout the body in a psychosomatic way. If the leader is domineeringly autocratic, watch out for a number of despots further down the food chain.

That is why Christ is regarded as the head (Ephesians 4:15), although note the flex in the metaphor as 1 Corinthians 12:16-7 identifies the eyes, ears and nose as mapped against human members! Banks writes, "the title arché, ruler, head or leader—often possessing in Greek a sense of legality or rank—never refers to individuals within communities, but significantly to Christ himself."[12] A leader is simply part of the body but tends to live up to the expectations placed on them. In relation to the church minister, Tidball contends, "Only as the unbiblical elevation of the clergyman is rejected and the biblical incorporation of the minister into the body takes place can the minister and his family receive the care they need."[13] First, the minister must remove the mask. You cannot do it all yourself, especially in youth work and ministry.

Whatever you have on your J.D., You are not the head! Some church leaders will refer to themselves as *under-shepherds* to remind themselves that Christ is the head, and the Good Shepherd of the flock (John 10:11). This isn't a bad thing to do, but even as an under-shepherd, youth pastor, gapper, volunteer or willing parent, don't get trapped into believing that you are indispensable. And not just to the teenagers. Mary had been struggling with her involvement in the youth ministry, but as I talked with her about the demands of her work at the doctor's surgery, I counseled her to take a year off helping run the mid-week group. She protested:

10. Morris, *Flexible Church*, 65.
11. Fee, *Corinthians*, 602.
12. Banks, *Paul's Idea of Community*, 135.
13. Tidball, *Skilful Shepherds*, 321.

"But that will leave just you and your wife!"

That confirmed the decision. She had pushed herself to the brink of burn-out so that she wouldn't let the team down. You can't buy that kind of loyalty and commitment, but you can abuse it. We forced her to take care of herself, and subsequently began to consider implementing one-year agreements for all volunteers, so that they had a ministry "out" without the emotional strings.

(Under) Shepherd. Vicar. Leader. Worker. Minister. Pastor. Co-ordinator. All of them indicate a one-way flow, towards those you work with, and the culture that we create can be toxic. I was at a large leader's conference, and the worship leader encouraged people to come down to be prayed for. I knew the dial was on empty, and I made to get out of my chair. Simultaneously, one of my colleagues commented with the sarcasm dripping:

"This is so formulaic. You could have predicted the worship, and how they always do the response like this. And I bet it's the same people who go forward at every conference . . . "

I succumbed to the adult peer-pressure and remained in my seat; in my need. Pride. I know leaders who are always there for people, and brilliant in crisis, but never show weakness themselves, who gave up going up for prayer many years ago. We have plenty of superheroes out there in youth work and ministry, busy rescuing the world one teenager at a time, not realising that the scrapes they pick up on the way need tending to, and there are some open sores that actually need time and space to heal.

Alfred: "Do you want to talk about how you're feeling right now?"

Lego Batman: "I don't talk about feelings, Alfred. I don't have any, I've never seen one. I'm a night-stalking, crime-fighting vigilante, and a heavy metal rapping machine. I don't feel anything emotionally, except for rage. 24/7, 365, at a million percent. And if you think that there's something behind that, then you're crazy."[14]

Ministers who never get ministered to, live in a lonely place, not too dissimilar to the Batcave. And it's not simply lonely—it's really stupid, feeling like a martyr for the gospel when all you have done is isolate yourself from the body. You do not sit above. You are not the head. You lead amongst.

---

14. McKay, *The Lego Batman Movie*.

Beyond the Nip and Tuck
THE TOTAL YOUTH WORKER IS PLURAL

For many youth work students, placement is a steep learning curve where their weaknesses are exposed. There is often frustration, coupled with a desire to grow. I take the party-pooper line: Give up. You are unlikely to become an extrovert if you have strong introvert tendencies, or suddenly become Little Miss Patient when you have lived for 24 years with ADHD. Rod Woods contends that "effective leadership requires that we focus on our strengths and not on our weaknesses."[15] So quit those lessons on extroversion and patience, and learn from Belbin, King David and Paul in doing two things:

1. Pour energy into your strengths, and invest in the strengths of others, and,
2. Compensate for, or manage your weaknesses by surrounding yourself with people who are gifted in ways that you are not.

We have bought into a false model, although it enjoyed some success on the soccer field, with the Dutch team, Ajax, masters of what was called *totaalvoetbal* (total football / soccer), winning all 46 home games in the 1972-73 season. For those who don't care for soccer, feel free to skip the next three diagrams. Totaalvoetbal "is a style of play where all 10 outfield players are comfortable in any position. [. . .] The only player with a fixed position is the goalkeeper, with defenders, midfielders and strikers all free to interchange, taking advantage of space left by the opposition."[16]

---

15. Woods, *Freed to Lead*, 89.
16. Coggin, "Total Football."

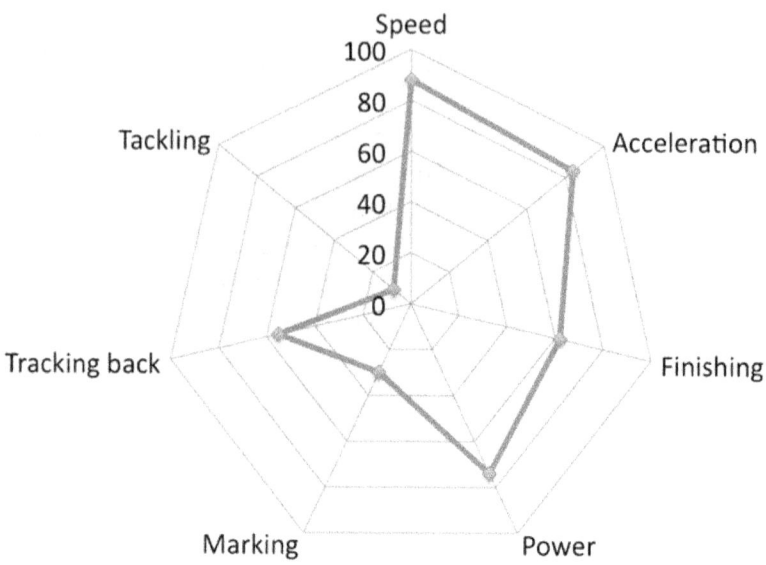

Figure 15: Forward Spider-Web Chart

Figure 15 shows a simple spider-web chart for a forward. Her primary attributes are speed and acceleration with finishing a touch low for playing at the top level. That said, there have been a number of excellent strikers who have lacked a typically desired attribute. Former Manchester United star, Dimitar Berbatov, confessed, "I've never been among the fastest players, I like to hold the ball, this is my style."[17] But here our forward has minimal defensive skills.

---

17. Dimitar Berbatov, quoted in Heneage, "Berbatov gains the space to flourish.".

Beyond the Nip and Tuck

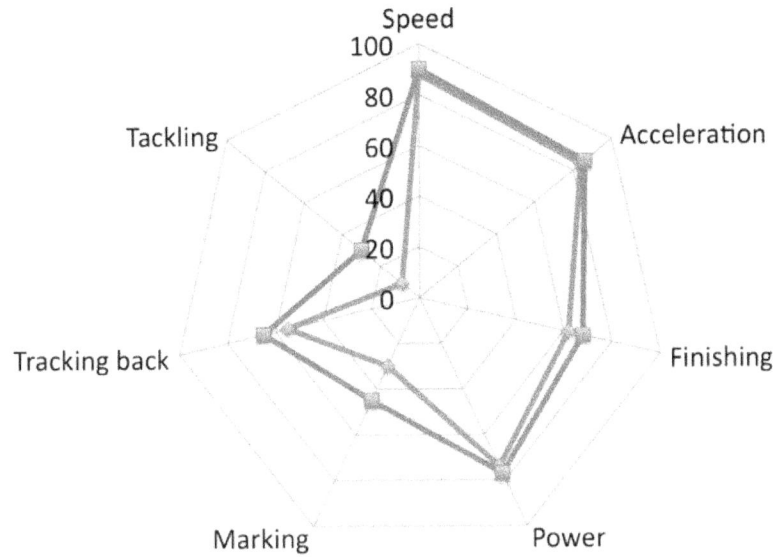

Figure 16: "Total Football" Forward Spider-Web Chart

This represents the hypothetical result of total football, with energy poured into developing the player holistically. In real terms, it will take far more effort and dedicated coaching to raise the defensive attributes to useful levels, and while there may be some improvement in the offensive attributes, they are sacrificed for a more rounded player. You can imagine our forward saying,

"Coach, why are you never letting me do some target practice, and take penalties? I've never been strong in tackles and never will be!"

I'm with her.

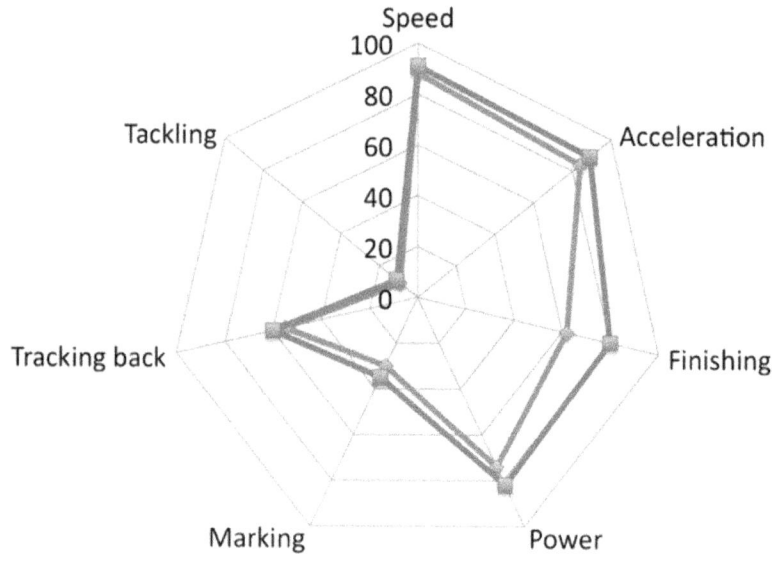

Figure 17: Focused Development Forward Spider-Web Chart

Figure 17 stands as chief antagonist to total football. To take speed from 90 to 92 takes a significant amount of sprint training and muscle work, while plenty of time with static and moving targets will improve finishing to a more acceptable level. Rather than attempt to improve every area, focus development effort on the skills that the role desperately needs.

We have an unhealthy obsession with the holistic, making it the holy grail of ministry, yet the holistic should be about the team, not the individual. The Pauline letters were written to churches, yet we often read them as to us as individuals. So where does the person fit? As part of the body. As wrestler-turned-actor, The Rock, aka Dwayne Johnson used to say, "Know your role, shut your mouth." When we work from a place of calling, terms and conditions seem almost irrelevant. You cannot think of doing anything that could make you feel more fulfilled. Yet the converse is also true: if you consistently operate in an area outside of your primary gift, role or even personality type, you will run dry and not last for the long haul.

Stop working harder. Many fall for that misleading and seemingly Christian work ethic. They treat long hours in ministry like spiritual air miles. Rather, work smarter. Eugene Peterson, author of *The Message* paraphrase, informed the church board that as pastor he would not be attending board meetings.[18] Outrageous? More like a man who knew and operated out of his calling, releasing both his gifts and theirs. Youth workers could learn something from Peterson's clarity over expectations, and refusal to bow down to the hero worship so many want to give. If I asked you how you were doing, would you want to tell me how busy you are? Underneath the status symbol that busyness has become, fighting fires in church is a full-time job and leaves most people worn out. There is a better way.

THINKING SYSTEMS

Fighting fires is important. Any destruction to property or people whether physically, intellectually, emotionally or spiritually should be abhorred. But your time would be better-spent long term by addressing the root cause of the blaze. Rather than focus on the cliques that have formed, turn your attention to the structures that have fostered the inward, exclusivity of the group. There's a story of a care home where residents who used a particular washbasin knew that there was the chance of an electric shock. The staff didn't know why sometimes a resident got a shock and other times they didn't. This intermittent nature led to a general acceptance. If you used that sink you took a risk, and they would simply treat the poor soul post-shock as and when it happened. Like me, you probably wonder why no one called out an electrician. Finally, when some of the rooms were renovated and the place rewired (it had not been touched since the 1960s), a frayed wire was discovered in the cupboard, that dangled close to the pipe work. When the cupboard was fully loaded with linen, the live wire would touch the metal.

While extreme, this acceptance reflects our own of situations that should be unacceptable, but while our focus is on the events rather than the systems, we will continue to patch people up, tend to the bruised and burnt out, try to find balance . . . and fight fires.

So much of what I have already written pushes you to consider the systems of caring for workers, relationships with the church leadership and the way in which we create a culture in which great youth work can be done. There are two revelations about the body imagery that can easily get missed: The relationship of the parts to each other, and the role of the ligaments.

---

18. For an insightful view of pastoral ministry, see Peterson, "The Business of Making Saints," 20-28.

Looking Good Naked

A new kind of relationship

One of my favorite writers is a German theologian called Jürgen Moltmann, although I don't agree with everything he says, for example, on social trinitarianism. He had a big idea that, "From first to last, and not merely in the epilogue, Christianity is eschatology, is hope, forward looking and forward moving, and therefore also revolutionizing and transforming the present."[19] The body imagery gives a sense of the future, with Ephesians 4:12-13 pointing out that leadership is given to "prepare God's people for service, so that the body of Christ may be built up until we all reach unity . . . and become mature." The Greek for mature here is *teleion*, which is often translated as perfect, for example, Matthew 5:48 "Be perfect *(teleios)* as your heavenly Father is perfect *(teleios),*" and carries the sense of purpose, or goal. Verse 15 adds that we will "grow up into Him who is the head (Jesus)." Youth ministry is concerned with maturity, accompanying young people through adolescence and into adulthood, growing in faith, in confidence, in abilities and empathy.

The danger is that we buy in to the kind of maturity and set of goals that the West venerates. Freedom is in vogue, but as a very individualistic pursuit, epitomized by the new paradigm Disney Princess, Elsa, who in her hit single, *Let it Go* equated a lack of rules as freedom.[20]

We idolize the individual, and if anything encroaches on our personal space, we feel restricted—unfree. Moltmann calls this freedom as domination—the ability to self-determine without being interfered with by others—and suggests that it is in some ways subhuman. Think about that the next time your tweenagers belt out the track acapella. His second definition of freedom is a direct challenge to this narcissistic pursuit: free communities. He contends that a "free society is not a collection of private, free individuals [but] a community in solidarity [w]here people intervene on one another's behalf."[21] A friend who has a young child commented on how they just want some "me time". I know what they mean, but profoundly disagree with what is being said. This hyperactive child is not a restriction on your freedom! By choosing to have a child / get involved in youth ministry / become part of a team, you are willingly opening yourself up to others. This is good but will cost you. Becoming a father made me realize just how

---

19. Moltmann, *Theology of Hope*, 2.
20. Go ahead and listen to the pre-chorus again!
21. Moltmann, *God for a Secular Society*, 158.

Beyond the Nip and Tuck

selfish and individualistic I am, and it has challenged my capacity to love and see my children as an extension of who I am, rather than as a boundary to my experience. In freedom as community, others become an extension of the self, and add a richness that you could not achieve on your own.

The body has many parts, but they are not atomized, as Moltmann would put it. They are joined together. They extend the experience of each other and work towards the common good (1 Corinthians 12:7). The weaker parts are honored as indispensable (1 Corinthians 12:22), which is an outrageous idea in the market-driven world in which we live, where you are judged by your performance. We need those that the world overlooks.

Derek was a shadow of his former self, having birthed the youth ministry at church back in his day. At 72 illness had taken its toll on his body, but not his spirit. With slurred speech and Parkinson's shakes, he recognized that he could no longer muck in on a Friday night, but desperately wanted to be involved. Derek began a youth prayer team, sending texts on his oversized mobile to nearly two dozen people, in response to regular, live updates from our ministry. 1 Corinthians 12:23 found an echo in his work. "The parts that are unpresentable are treated with special modesty," and heaven rejoices. Derek will be remembered as a hero of the faith in that town.

Don't miss that it's not us who put these "kingdom dream teams" together. In fact, on closer reflection on the text of verse 13, "Paul's primary alteration of the body metaphor is the designation of the church as not just a body but Christ's body, composed by the Spirit."[22] God arranges the body "as he sees fit" (v18) and distributes his gifts likewise (Romans 12:6). Not only is the body put together by the Spirit, it is also filled by the Spirit. Verse 7 draws on a rare expression in the Greek around the public manifestation of the Spirit given to each member for the common good, revealing that "the animating power and purpose is *one*, even if phenomena in the public domain take diverse forms."[23] If that was not persuasive enough, Paul goes on in verse 13 to speak of members being "baptized by one Spirit" and "given the one Spirit to drink" and in doing so pushed against the fractious community at Corinth, endorsing "the notion of a dynamic experience of the Holy Spirit which transcended boundaries of race, class, culture, and status."[24] Ours is a deeply spiritual relationship with one another, and being

---

22. Morris, *Flexible Church*, 130.
23. Thiselton, *The First Epistle to the Corinthians*, 936.
24. Thiselton, *The First Epistle to the Corinthians*, 999.

filled with the spirit is corporate, for the building up and enabling of His body. Ephesians 4:3 calls us to put effort into maintaining the unity that is already in play through the Spirit. Moltmann would likely critique us for reading the bible as atomized individuals, claiming for ourselves what is actually meant for the body. In fact, "Among the 90 New Testament references where "Holy Spirit" and "you" appear in the same verse, the only times the Holy Spirit is given to a singular "you" is Mary at the Annunciation (Luke 1:35) and the Apostle Paul at his conversion with Ananias (Acts 9:17)."[25] We need to re-read the New Testament in light of this.

Leaders are ligaments

Factoid of the day: the human body has close to 1,000 tough bands of tissue known as ligaments, with the majority found in your extremities.

What's fascinating is how conversant Paul was with these ideas back in the first century, noting that the body is joined and held together by ligaments, whose job it is to support and facilitate. That sounds a lot like leadership to me. But leadership isn't restricted to the brain or heart—it is most effective when it is seen near or at the interface with the world. While I applaud the apostles for prioritising prayer and Scripture in Acts 6, they inadvertently moved themselves away from the action, and handed the task of serving at tables to others. What's interesting is that they delegated *authority* to the men and women there, to recognize leaders from within their number, rather than just delegate *jobs* to people. The seven chosen were not content to keep the machinery ticking over—they took risks and led by example. What you begin to see is leadership at every level, and the center of gravity moving away from the core in Jerusalem, with Acts 9—11 chronicling the shift of focus to "all Judea and Samaria," prepping for world mission (Acts 1:8). It's an incredible image that challenges the leader-centric world we live in. Leaders release leaders, and facilitate the ministry, not pull it all off in their own strength. Lesslie Newbigin writes, 'the priestly people needs a ministering priesthood to sustain and nourish it [. . .] The business of leadership is precisely to enable, encourage, and sustain the activity of all the members.'[26] Interestingly, Paul seems intentional in avoiding the words *leader* and *leadership* when talking about the congregations, opting

---

25. McGarry, *A Biblical Theology*, 90-1.
26. Newbigin, *The Gospel in a Pluralist Society*, 235.

to speak of "co-workers" and of people serving or ministering (from the greek *diakonia*).

Wearing spandex morph suits not only raises safeguarding concerns, but have-a-go heroes "pay a heavy personal price: alienation, feelings of failure, stress-induced illness, and early death. Organisations and institutions [and churches] suffer and splutter because we ask too much of our leaders and not enough of ourselves."[27] Let's not ignore those with special powers like The Hulk, or just plain heroic ability and grit like Batman. Create room for individual talent, but locate it in the context of inter-dependent teams where the members compensate and work for one another. In every-member-ministry language, "From [Christ] the whole body, *joined and held together by every supporting ligament*, grows and builds itself up in love, as each part does its work" (Eph4:16, emphasis mine).

That's total youth work.

In the following four short chapters, we will be reimagining the four core values of youth work noted in chapter one in light of developing a healthy ecclesiology.

FOR REFLECTION AND DISCUSSION:

1. How healthy is your body image? Are the weaker elements given room to grow, and how might you compensate for your own weaknesses?

2. Map out what it would look like with a team comprised of mini-yous. Talk with a friend about what would be better, and what would be worse if there were a number of "you" around.

3. Are those with leadership positions and gifts acting like ligaments or trying to be the head? What would it look like if more time was invested joining, holding and supporting?

4. How much of your time is spent fighting fires, and how much developing and maintaining systems? How might you become more systems orientated?

---

27. Bolman and Deal, *Leading with the Soul*, 62.

7

Let them go

Why we need voluntary communities

Me: "I don't want your teenager coming to the youth group on Sundays."*

*Pregnant pause. I try to gauge the parental response. Anger? Confusion? . . . do I detect a slither of relief?

The contention is that without the voluntary participation of the young person, "there can be no youth work and ministry,"[1] because the relationship between the youth worker and the young person is based on a voluntary contract. In a similar vein Davies defines youth work in terms of young people "[choosing] to be involved,"[2] but sadly appreciates that young people are sometimes required to attend youth clubs.[3] Young people must be able to opt in or opt out of a programme. It is freedom of choice. Jeffs writes that "Youth work is not an enforced activity; it is about working with young people on their own terms. Young people do not have to go to a youth activity, they can decide whether or not they would like to join in. This idea of voluntary participation distinguishes youth work from other disciplines."[4]

Andy Hillier painted a bleak picture in the UK where, "Increasingly, youth workers are expected to work with young people who have not asked to be there or, more to the point, might not want to be. In schools, on youth

---

1. Brierley, *Joined Up*, 61.
2. Davies, "What do we mean by youth work?" 1-2.
3. Davies, "What do we mean by youth work?" 2.
4. Jeffs, "Something to give and much to learn," 156.

offending programmes and in custody young people are being "referred" to youth workers without expressing any willingness to do so."[5] It may be work with young people, but it's not authentic youth work.

Sam wasn't the first, nor would she be the last, but took the prize for the most awkward. She would come into the youth group on a Sunday morning with a face of thunder.

I really wanted to state the obvious: "Let me guess: you don't want to be here." She could sit for the hour saying absolutely nothing, staring into an invisible abyss behind my head, or alternatively become the chief architect of mayhem, ensuring that everyone leaves at the end feeling worse than when they started. We challenged her, cheered her, chivvied her . . . and gave up. None of my techniques gained results, no matter how manipulative I was with rewards and punishments. Skinner's behaviorism theory was quickly disproved and abandoned by the team! And so to the awkward conversation with mum, narrated at the start of the chapter. There was a measure of relief, mixed with disappointment and anger, as every week they had the same row at 10:15am over attending the group.

I now try to have this conversation much earlier with parents, and it does work. I tell them that I do not want them to bring their son or daughter to the youth group until *they want* to be there. Before parental outrage kicks in, I offer that I will meet with their child outside of church, and work to integrate them into relationships with other young people and adults. Kirsty asked me to do something with her son, Jacob, who was completely disengaged from church and getting involved in with young people who were engaged in low-level criminal activity. My first step was to meet him down the park with a soccer ball and explore where he was at and the questions he had while we booted the ball back and forth.

Participation has also acted as a safeguard for us on a number of occasions. Doing Christian small groups, teens often invite their friends, and when we have used Youth Alpha material (complete with yummy puddings—you know who you are if you are reading this . . . thank you!), we have seen small groups emerge with up to 70% un-churched, not-yet-Christians involved. There is no hard sell or compulsion to believe what we do. We found out that Melissa's dad had a real go at her one night when she got back from KABOOM.[6]

---

5. Hillier, "The Erosion of Voluntary Participation."
6. Well, it's better than calling it Ig:nite or Eliv8!

Dad: "I don't want you going there every week—they're brain-washing you."

Melissa: "Dad, that's not fair. Mike said tonight not to just take their word for it, and make up your own minds."

(Ka)Boom.

I'm so glad that was how we rolled as a team. We cannot make people believe what we believe. We hold that the Holy Spirit is the one who convicts of sin and righteousness, not us (John 16:8), and a core belief for Christians is that humans have free-will (put down your predestination weapons for one moment!). It is a tragedy when churches tell people what to believe. Brierley adds that "those who have confidence in the gospel have no need to manipulate or coerce young people into accepting the message of Christ."[7]

A voluntary community creates an atmosphere where people want to be involved, and feel able to come and go without coercion, yet, just like with members of a body, people should be missed when they are not there. Our Western cultures are increasingly marked by loneliness, with almost one in three British young people reporting feeling lonely often or all the time,[8] heightened ironically by the social platforms that promise social connection. In a rich piece of research into the experiences of young people the authors note, "Loneliness is in part an abjected and stigmatised state. There are powerful social and psychological pressures to appear socially successful, and loneliness is thus something that young people, like others, may seek to hide or deny, and find difficult to talk about."[9] Loneliness is not combatted effectively through distraction and activity. You can feel lonely in a crowd and not want to turn up even when you are depended upon. Steven Bonner writes into what he calls performance-based acceptance, suggesting it "is particularly damaging when it comes from trusted adults." He demands that, "our churches must be places of refuge and safety, not another system of adult-centred performance-driven agendas that must be carefully negotiated by the growing adolescent."[10] On reflection, I am guilty of facilitating events and activities where young people's credibility and social status is put on the line, and vigilance is needed to ensure people are missed, not because of what they bring, but because of who they are—intrinsically valued as members of the body and part of God's family.

7. Brierley, *Joined Up*, 11.
8. Majoribanks and Bradley, *The Way We Are Now*, 15.
9. Batsleer, Duggan, McNicol, Spray and Angel, *Loneliness Connects Us*, 11.
10. Bonner, "Understanding the Changing Adolescent," 31, 35.

1 John 3 declares, "how great the love the Father has lavished on us that we should be called children of God—and that is what we are." John goes on: "We love, because he first loved us" (1 John 4:19).

Three years later, Sam was Little Miss Consistent, and would often turn up to church meetings, regardless of whether her peers were there or not. She had bought in to the vision of the church and was discovering her place in the body, that she mattered, missed when not there, and how she could relate to others. We had begun to help her find answers to those questions that define the experience of adolescence for many without coercion, bribery or heavy-handed approaches.[11]

The front door is essential, creating multiple opportunities for involvement without needing force, but voluntary participation demands you have fire exits that people can leave through without having to wrestle past the Hulk or Thor. This means being confident in your body image that numbers do not define you. Sometimes young people need to leave, and you can either enable them to do so with dignity, or act in a way that is detrimental to future growth and potential reconnections with the body.

The badly titled story *The Prodigal Son*[12] captures the love that sits behind the decision to let them go, and takes it to a whole new level, because in the story, found only in Luke's Gospel, it's not a youth pastor—young person relationship, but father to son. That the younger son's request for his inheritance is granted early is astonishing. He has effectively told his dad that he might as well be dead, and rather than put his son on the naughty step, the father lets him go. He is well aware of the vices and threats that his son will face, but love compels him to take his hands off. Forcing involvement backfires, if not in activity then definitely in attitude.

VOLUNTARILY OR PNEUMATOLOGICALLY CONNECTED?

John Locke contended that, "A Church, then, I take to be a voluntary society of men, joining themselves together of their own accord in order to the public worshiping of God [. . .] I say it is a free and voluntary society. Nobody is born a member of any church."[13] While many would agree with this statement, it must be more nuanced than simply a collection of individuals

---

11. See Clark, "The changing face of Adolescence," 55.
12. *Lost Son* and *Lovesick Father* are just as bad!
13. Locke, "A Letter Concerning Toleration," in *On Politics and Education*, 27.

choosing to commit to each other, lest we end up thinking we can do this in our own strength after all in some kind of avengers endgame. My suggestion here is that while voluntary relationships must be facilitated at every single access point for young people, we tend to put the focus on the human connection. I have heard countless parents encourage their teens to attend based on perceived friendship groups, essentially playing on a fear of missing out. Yet the focus of this book has been the metaphor of the Church understood as the "body of Christ in which all members however different [. . .] must share the common life, complementing and helping one another precisely by their differences."[14] This common life does not depend on us, but as both 1 Corinthians 12 and Ephesians 4:15-16 remind us,

> "We belong to the body of Christ. By the grace of God in Christ we are members of the body of which Christ is the head. The sinews of God's Word and Spirit hold us together. Our unity is not sure because of our hold on one another. God's hold alone is sure. And God alone holds the church."[15]

The primary relationship is not one to another, although this is a natural and common outworking: it is to Christ. It's his body, after all. We belong not to each other, but to God. The idea that we manipulate attendance based on the human relationships is flawed therefore for two reasons: it cuts against the voluntary principle, and more significantly theologically, it exchanges the mystical concept of church for a sociological one.

In an incredible plot twist, Jesus demonstrates the voluntary principle, drawing on the metaphor of the good shepherd: "I know my sheep and they know me [. . .] and I lay my life down for my sheep [. . .] of my own accord" (John 10:15, 18). As those who work with young people, modelling that kind of self-sacrifice speaks volumes.

FOR REFLECTION AND DISCUSSION:

1. How easy is it for a young person to leave your youth group? What kind of pressure might they feel?
2. How do you demonstrate that you miss people when they are not there?

---

14. Lewis, *Letters of C.S. Lewis*, 224.
15. Jinkins, "The 'Gift' of the Church" in *Evangelical Ecclesiology*, 188.

3. Consider what strategies you have in place for young people who do not fit the profile of the groups you offer.

8

Fill them up

Why we need empowering communities

EVERY SUPERHERO SCRIPT HAS a cast of villains, whose primary role it would seem is to leave a community in such difficulties that only someone with superhuman characteristics will do. If the community fails, grab some gaffer-tape, rig up the spotlight, and illuminate the skies. But corporate vigilance is called for to keep the superhero at the job-center. Paul, writing to the church in Corinth, reminds the community that "we are not unaware of [satan's] schemes" (2 Corinthians 2:11). Knowing the villains is over half the battle, and two villains stand out from the others:

Villain One: Entertainment

Encourages dependence, babysitting young people through adolescence on behalf of the church "that is cash rich and time poor."[1] Young people are distracted, and not encouraged to grow up towards independence, and, ultimately, to interdependence.

Villain Two: Fear factor

The problem with working yourself out of a job is that if you are successful, you end up unemployed! A pastor told me that he didn't worry about giving

---

1. Ward, *Growing up evangelical*, 199.

Fill them up

people with greater giftings opportunity to take center stage. He was right. And it was evident from his actions.

Once a young person participates, the extent to which they are able to achieve largely depends on you and me providing the space for them, returning to the image of the sweepers in curling, from the preface. The answer is gloriously simple and takes little more than a surface reading of Ephesians 4:11-16. God has distributed giftings to all to facilitate growth in order that the body of Christ might be built up. Young people must be considered full participants in this.

Roger Hart defined participation as "the process of sharing decisions which affect one's life and the life of the community in which ones lives" and his Ladder of Participation sets out levels of youth participation (Figure 18).[2] "The strength of the ladder lies in its iconic familiarity and simplicity, yet these are also limitations,"[3] and there are certainly critics.[4] That said, it does provide a useful tool in analysing the extent to which young people are involved.

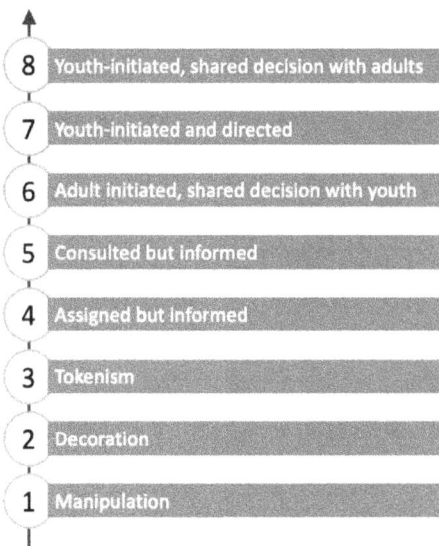

Figure 18: Ladder of Participation[5]

---

2. Hart, *Children's Participation*, 5.
3. Hart's Ladder in *"Children and Young People's Participation,"* 15.
4. Davies, "Participation," 23.
5. Hart's Ladder, in *"Children and Young People's Participation,"* 16.

Based on this model, some of what passes for the integration of youth ministry within the local church is what Hart might describe as tokenism, manipulation and decoration.[6]

The following chart is by Adam Fletcher, who has built on Hart's work (which, in turn, was built on a model of citizen participation!). I have added a fourth column to indicate risk elements for the worker to consider.

Description	Challenge	Reward	Risk
1. Adults manipulate youth	Youth forced to attend without regard to interest.	Experience of involving youth and rational for continuing activities.	Risks resentment from young people, who are a burden to the adults. Youth are lost as soon as they gain power over their involvement.
2. Adults use youth to decorate their activities	The presence of youth is treated as all that is necessary without reinforcing active involvement.	A tangible outcome demonstrating thinking about youth voice.	The culture says that children should be seen and not heard. Risks youth experiencing a 'glass ceiling' effect.
3. Adults tokenize youth	Young people are used inconsequentially by adults to reinforce the perception that youth are involved.	Validates youth attendance without requiring the work to go beyond that.	Risks youth feeling used by the adult community, who consider that they have accommodated young people sufficiently.
4. Youth inform adults	Adults do not *have* to let youth impact their decisions.	Youth can impact adult-driven decisions or activities.	Risk disappointed youth when ideas go nowhere, and, if sustained, risk disengagement.
5. Adults actively consult youth while they're involved	Youth only have the authority that adults grant them, and are subject to adult approval.	Youth can substantially transform adults' opinions, ideas, and actions.	Risk of lip service being paid to consultations.

6. Fletcher, "Ladder of Young People's Participation."

Description	Challenge	Reward	Risk
6. Youth are fully equal with adults while they're involved. This is a 50/50 split of authority, obligation, and commitment.	There isn't recognition for the specific developmental needs or representation opportunities for youth. Without receiving that recognition youth loose interest and may become disengaged quickly.	Youth can experience full power and authority, as well as the experience of forming basic youth/adult partnerships.	Risk of role ambiguity and frustration for both adults and young people.
7. Young person-driven activities do not include adults in positions of authority; rather, they are there to support youth in passive roles.	Youth operate in a vacuous situation where the impact of their larger community isn't recognised by them. Young person-driven activities may not be seen with the validity of co-led activities, either.	Developing complete ownership of their learning allows youth to drive the educational experience with a lot of effectiveness. Youth experience the potential of their direct actions upon themselves, their peers, and their larger community.	Risk of expecting too much of young people, and miss out on true partnerships, alienating adults.
8. Youth have full equity with adults. This may be a 40/60 split, or 20/80 split when it's appropriate. All are recognised for their impact and ownership of the outcomes.	Requires conscious commitment by all participants to overcoming all barriers.	Creating structures to support differences can establish safe, supportive learning environments, ultimately recreating the climate and culture in communities.	Risk of damaging young person through over-exposure without emotional maturity. Risk of missing outcomes.

Figure 19: Youth Voice Rubric[7]

Levels 1 to 3 are the reason why I personally will never do another youth-led service. The first question should be to ask who the activity is actually for. To answer this, consider where the impetus for the youth-led service is coming from, and who benefits from it. My vision is to integrate young people into the body so that it can grow into maturity. The following is part of a service in which I was the only adult voice, with the exception of

7. Fletcher, "Youth Voice Rubric," with 4th column by Andy du Feu, August 2013.

Jane, who was heard through whispered cues directed to young people on a regular basis.

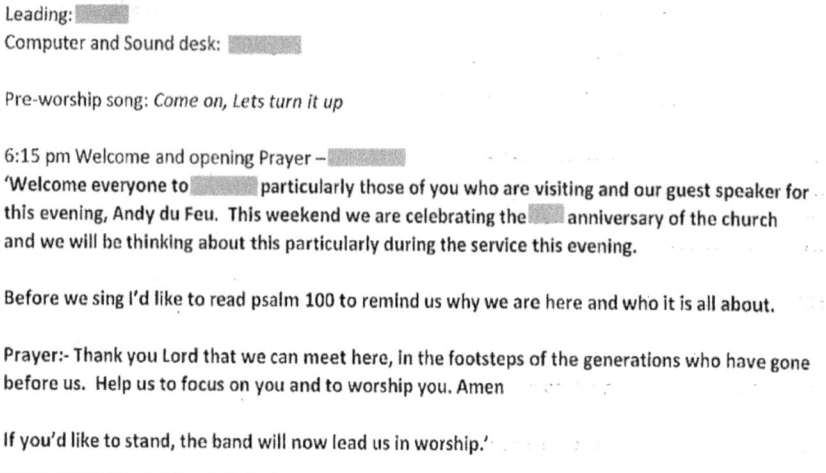

Figure 20: Youth - Led Service Plan

At 6:15, Seth knew that he had to stand up and read the welcome. Only Jane had not appreciated that when the script said, "I'd like to read psalm 100," Seth wouldn't join the dots and pick up a Bible. Sadly, that night there was no Bible reading to "remind us who it's about," as the script indicated. Seth, in classic monotone, read the whole paper with zero attention to punctuation. Try it yourself:

> "Before we sing I'd like to read psalm 100 to remind us why we are here and who it is all about prayer thank you Lord that we can meet here in the footsteps of the generations who have gone before us help us to focus on you and to worship you amen if you'd like to stand the band will now lead us in worship."

To many, it looked like youth empowerment. "Check it out, everyone—he's leading a service!" I actually watched people go up to Seth after the service to say how well he had done. But that night, the church spectacularly failed Seth, setting him up to believe a lie, and miss the whole point of what they were trying to model. Yes, they had pushed past levels 1—3 (although 3 was present), but they experienced the risk of empowerment seen in Figure 21.

Fill them up

I would love to say that I have never made these mistakes. Emma was an outstanding 15-year-old girl who pioneered our first peer-led cell group. Naturally confident like Tony Stark and as organized as Pepper Potts, she was the complete package. We left her to pick material and call the first session. I turned up to the first meeting, and it was flawless. I made a couple of encouraging remarks and left after half an hour. We decided to give her space over the next month without us interfering, and sat back, congratulating ourselves on our ability to release young people in ministry. A text shattered the illusion, asking us for help as the group were rebelling, and some hadn't attended for a fortnight. We turned up on the Tuesday night, to a room populated by empty chairs. Emma occupied a couch to herself, head buried in her hands. In a position of authority, she had become a bossy dictator, and the group had voted with their feet. We failed her.

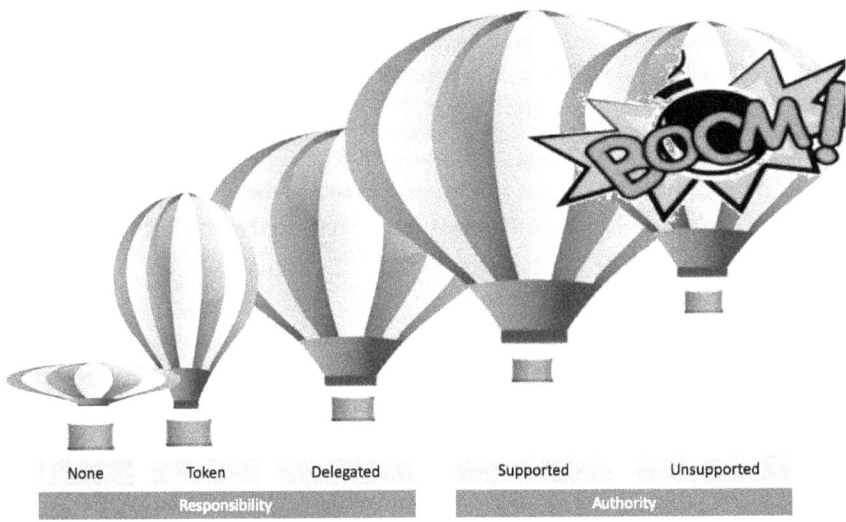

Figure 21: Limits to empowerment[8]

This captures how giving young people token responsibility starts to inflate the balloon. Others see empowerment, but there isn't enough to get the balloon to fly. With delegated, and then supported levels of authority, a young person can really grow. Jamie Cutteridge, former editor of Youthwork Magazine, took vital supplies to the migrants stuck on the Calais border, who hope to get into the UK. With him were experienced youth workers... and young people. Brilliant. But without support, the likelihood

---

8. Balloon designed by Freepik.com

of damage increases. For example, a young person who has responded out of deep empathetic concern might take risks that a youth worker would not. There is an almost mythical story from an urban youth ministry on the East Coast about an 18-year-old intern who was sent home when he was discovered handling drugs for a local dealer. Somehow, the desire to connect with young people crossed a line, driven by a deeper need to be accepted and liked. They were out there, an empowered youth worker, about to torpedo the ministry they were aiming to expand. There must be the supportive framework and structures in place to ensure that empowerment benefits the young person. Without this, releasing people is really casting them adrift.

Len Kageler often says that the key factor in the growth in his youth ministry was the decision to involve teenagers, and James Emery White delivers the hulk-smash: "Platform them!"[9] Lawrence contends that "the practice of youth-led ministry creates a saturating counterculture."[10] I agree, but not in isolation from the body, disconnected from other members. Seth and Emma were visibly *platformed*, but in reality were hung out to dry. Figure 20 reflects how empowerment can backfire with little support. Balswick et al paint the bigger picture of empowerment, as the "process of instilling confidence, teaching, guiding, equipping, challenging, strengthening and building up children to become all that they are meant to be."[11] And this isn't simply about putting them on a stage. That can merely propagate a celebrity culture. If the limit of our empowerment is a youth band, young preacher or peer-led group, we will never realize the potential of the body. But does this spell the end of the nativity play with the 4-year-old shepherd who forgets his lines and kisses the girl angel as she tries to dance gracefully behind the motionless frames of Mary and Joseph? Of course not. You will find that great youth work practice incorporates several rungs of the ladder at any one time, working with many different young people.

As a pastor I was able to advocate for young people, as well as muck in with the youth team. We had a fourteen-year-old and a seventeen-year-old involved with the sound desk and visual media, and several mid-to-late teens on the preaching rota and integrated into the regular worship team. One Sunday night I looked over and saw Chris, the 16-year-old who had just preached, go up to Steve, a successful businessman, and share then pray

---

9. Emery White, *What they didn't teach you*, 77.
10. Lawrence, *Jesus Centred Youth Ministry*, 83.
11. Balswick, *Relationship-Empowerment*.

with him. I loved that our church community had that kind of atmosphere, where younger could minister to older, and vice-versa. It requires

> "an ideological shift [. . .] moving from "Youth as Consumers" (if we build it they will come—and then we can grow) to "Youth as Asked" (if we inform them of options, they will provide feedback—and then we can serve them better) to "Youth as Empowered" (if we partner with them in every segment of ministry, they will recognize need and response options—and then we can consciously put more and more decisions in their hands and facilitate their leadership."[12]

A former student and local youth pastor, Sam Pink, captured it well: "If you think empowering young people will lighten the load for you, you've got it wrong." She is so right. Young people need the training and investment so they can succeed when platformed. Long after Omar had left the youth ministry, I discovered the reason that he had thrown in the towel. He was assisting 8-10-year olds with their home-work assignments, yet his reading age at 15 was pre-teen. His fragile ego was assaulted every single day that he was employed by us. No wonder the lure of quick money on the streets as a look out for dealers was more appealing than consistent income in an educational setting. I failed (again) because I didn't invest in Omar enough to assess where he was at academically.

Ephesians 4:12 is absolutely clear: people in positions have a responsibility to equip others so that they can take part in ministry. Yes, believe them into greatness, but kit them out with the right gear to take their place in body.

FOR REFLECTION AND DISCUSSION:

1. Are your young people consumers of a product or participants within a service?
2. What opportunities does your church or organisation provide for young people? Are they taken?
3. How could you develop this?

---

12. Berard, Penner and Bartlett, *Consuming Youth*, 153.

9

Clear their path
Why we need welcoming communities

EVERY SINGLE AVENGER HAS a reason to be the odd one out. Captain America wakes up to find he has no friends, and the world has changed somewhat, having been in deep freeze for 70 years. He's the all-American hero in an age of cynicism. Thor comes from a world where people walk up and over rainbows, and Bruce Banner is best left to himself. His alter-ego generally runs around naked, but for seriously elasticated yet shredded shorts.

When churches advertise for a superhero, they discover that youth workers come in a variety of styles, passions and giftings. The differences are needed, as young people rarely fit the cookie cutter either. When Phoebe arrived at the youth club, it was clear she meant business, destroying the ego of Rugby Football-mad Simon as she cut him down in a slide tackle. The older lads, who held quite chauvinistic views about gender roles, found themselves back peddling desperately.

What's the most random thing you have said to a young person?

Me: "That samurai sword—you're going to have to leave that here at the door. Weapons aren't allowed in the church."

There is no sensible reason such a combination of words should ever be uttered. Ellie was a regular at our open access club but was very much on the social fringe, being into Japanese Manga comics in a big way. When her friend was there, they would literally speak gibberish to each other all night. When alone, she would isolate herself—once discovered sitting underneath a pile of chairs in the dark. Connecting with her meant first offering a welcome—helped by listening to her interpretation of Manga, and doing my own research by watching *Dragon Ball Z*.

IMITATING THE WELCOME

If verses 1-6 of Ephesians 4 are about the cohesion of the body, verse 7-13 are seemingly paradoxically about the diversity of the members. But the juxtaposition is satisfied by recognising that Christianity is not about uniformity but unity in diversity. Perhaps a better rendering of Paul's call in 1 Corinthians 11:1 to "imitate me as I imitate Christ" is to "imitate me *insofar as* I imitate Christ" (NLT). The danger with any superhero youth worker is that we do the first part really well, resulting in an army clad in replica morph suits. The body rejects uniformity, because Christ Himself graces each one of us uniquely. It's rooted in the imagery of Psalm 68 of a king returning from battle with the spoils of war distributed amongst the common people. Not only are gifts given, there are specific roles that people are appointed to, often referred to as the five-fold ministry of Apostles, Prophets, Evangelists, Pastors and Teachers. The final point is that the gifts are given to equip the body so that it can build itself up to maturity. When we place obstacles in the path of people because they don't fit our image, we deprive ourselves of the grace at work in their lives. That's why equality of opportunity exists—to remove barriers to access, and Christians should be market leaders in this, not perceived as bigoted haters.

Why? Because that is the imitation of Christ. To a culture in which kids were seen as insignificant, he said, "Let the little children come to me, for the kingdom of Heaven belongs to such as these" (Mark 10:14). To the religious leaders who distanced themselves from those who didn't match their standards of righteousness Jesus said, "I have come to call sinners" (Mark 2:17). Eating with tax collectors; embracing those with skin diseases; talking with prostitutes: the proof of welcome is so consistent that when the disciples saw Him talking with a woman by a well, they said nothing (John 4) despite the social rules that their rabbi was trampling over. The Bible records Jesus being indignant—angry about the barriers that people placed in the way of access to the kingdom of God.

But we are so good at creating barriers. I would always say that I am pro-equality of opportunity and have a welcome that extends beyond the newcomers meal, but my actions so often prove otherwise. We ran a 5-day version of *Slum Survivor*, with dozens of people involved in building their own habitat and surviving without things like smart phones, hair-straighteners, PlayStations and chocolate. What we didn't expect in a reasonably mild October was heavy snow. A reporter from the regional news heard about our story and came over with the TV crew and we featured for two nights running. The second night was brilliant, as the weather crew wanted to interview us and wrap the plight of 20 teenagers in a field into their weather report. I was asked to put forward two young people to be interviewed, and I chose Lucas and Georgia, both who were naturally confident and articulate, and those I thought would come over best—and not embarrass us.

It was one of my worst moments in youth work.

I refused access to young people who would have flourished with such an opportunity, and played it safe—for my benefit, not theirs. I regret the choice I made, as implicitly I informed the group of young people of what was acceptable and what was not.

INCLUSIVE OF THE EXCLUSIVE

Equality of opportunity is about addressing the power imbalance, something Jesus often upset as I suggest above. Yet there are clear tensions theologically. If you want to hold Jesus up as a poster model for inclusion, you need to either reconcile or ignore some of the more challenging moments, such as his purpose statement (I was sent only to the lost sheep of Israel) and dismissal of the woman's ethnicity (It is not right to toss the children's bread to the dogs) in Mark 7. What about Jesus telling a man that his wealth was a barrier to kingdom access. There is also the bigger issue of the truth claims about Jesus Himself.

How did Jesus self-identify? As the "way, the truth and the life. No-one comes to the Father except through me" (John 14:6). How did the early church understand these claims? Peter is clear: "there is salvation in no one else, for there is no other name under heaven given among men by which we must be saved" (Acts 4:12).

We operate exclusivity in every area of society, from private health care (excluding those without money) to height charts at fairground rides. Life is framed by being "in" or being "out". Yes, there is an exclusive message at the heart of the Christian faith, but all should be welcomed to it.

That's the scandal of Christianity. Ephesians 4:22-24 reveals this powerful paradigm:

> "those parts of the body that seem to be weaker are indispensable, 23 and the parts that we think are less honorable we treat with special honor. And the parts that are unpresentable are treated with special modesty . . . But God has put the body together . . ."

It is worth pausing at this point to realize that Paul did not speak into a cultural vacuum. What's known as the body politic was developed after Paul, but also preceded him. In 494 BC Menenius Agrippa (not the same as Herod Agrippa of Acts 12 or Julius Marcus Agrippa of Acts 26) told a fable to encourage the working class not to rise up against the Senate:

> "A commonwealth resembles in some measure a human body. [It] consists of many parts; and no one of their parts either has the same function or performs the same service as the others. [. . .] and the feet should say that the whole body rests on them; the hands that they ply the crafts; [. . .] the mouth, that it speaks [. . .] and then all these say to the belly, [. . .] "what do you do?""[1]

The correlation with the words of 1 Corinthians and Ephesians 4 is unmistakable. However, "whereas the political writers sought harmony through adherence to established hierarchies of power, Paul urges equal respect and appreciation for the parts of the body whose significance is usually discounted."[2] The political powers sought to defend the hegemony, but the body of Christ was to be different, building on the words of the master who modelled his own words in Matthew 20:26-28:

> "Jesus called them together and said, "You know that the rulers of the Gentiles lord it over them, and their high officials exercise authority over them. Not so with you. Instead, whoever wants to become great among you must be your servant, and whoever wants to be first must be your slave—just as the Son of Man did not come to be served, but to serve, and to give his life as a ransom for many.""

God's design is diversity in unity—the poor are welcomed to the feast alongside the rich. Morris goes further, contending that "Rather than urging those of lower status to remember their dependence on those of higher

---

1. This text is accessible from a number of places. This version is from http://penelope.uchicago.edu/Thayer/E/Roman/Texts/Dionysius_of_Halicarnassus/6D*.html.
2. Scott Nash, *1 Corinthians*, 362.

status, Paul exhorts those of higher status to remember their dependence on those of lower status."[3] That status can be real, or perceived. We took a group of rural teens to a large festival. They were like rabbits in headlights for the first day, and I will never forget the moment they came back to the tents, exclaiming, "We saw a bunch of chavs—and they were Christians!"

Their bewilderment betrayed their "in" or "out" worldview. But a healthy body image challenges the polarisation. Be careful here not to draw on texts such as Galatians 3:28, which declares, "There is neither Jew nor Gentile, neither slave nor free, nor male or female for you are all one in Christ Jesus." I've heard many youth talks where it has been said, "There is neither [in group] or [out group]" but this abuses the text. Chapter 3 demonstrates the futility of trying to be saved through your own strength, and the three categories are intentional, corresponding "to a number of Jewish formulas [. . .] as in the morning prayer in which the male Jew thanks God that he was not made a Gentile, a slave or a woman."[4] Bruce goes on to illustrate the lack of "distinction between Jews and Gentiles before God in respect either of their moral bankruptcy or of their need to receive his pardoning grace. The law-free gospel put both communities on one and the same level before God, so that 'in Christ' there was 'neither Jew nor Greek'"[5] The basic message is, if you are in Christ, regardless of your ethnic, social or physical status, you are heirs of the promise given to Abraham. The verse, in its context, is about salvation, not ministry! Clearly the binaries couldn't say, God-fearer nor God-hater" with Morris noting that, "Although the church was counterculturally inclusive in relation to social status and ethnicity, its identity as Christ's body excluded other religious affiliations."[6]

There are better ways to challenge the in-out worldview. Note the immense scenes in Revelation 7:9 where a countless "multitude from every nation, tribe, people and language" stood before Jesus. When we see the body of Christ cross cultural and ethnic lines here on earth, we capture a glimpse of that day.

---

3. Morris, *Flexible Church*, 131.
4. Bruce, *The Epistle to the Galatians*, 187.
5. Bruce, *The Epistle to the Galatians*, 188.
6. Morris, *Flexible Church*, 108.

RELIGION OR RELATIONSHIP?

One of my pet peeves is the false dichotomy that so many people create between religion and relationship. It's a phrase that is used to contrast a bureaucratic and oppressive system with some kind of organic relationship. The problem is, it's spoken in complete ignorance. First, Dulles writes that "Some of the objections to the institutional model [of church] can be answered if the institution is understood not in the abstractions of modern sociology, but in terms of what God "instituted" in Christ."[7] When the UK media speaks of "the church" they typically mean the Church of England hierarchy, rather than the local expression or the communion of the saints which is far more organic, although as we note, many have structures that essentially help them stay organised and working effectively.

Secondly, religion is far bigger than a set of rules (although it includes behavior and social organisation). Writing in TheGuardian, Karen Armstrong captures the linguistic limitation of how we use the word *religion*:

> "The Arabic word din signifies an entire way of life, and the Sanskrit dharma covers law, politics, and social institutions as well as piety. The Hebrew Bible has no abstract concept of "religion"; and the Talmudic rabbis would have found it impossible to define faith in a single word or formula, because the Talmud was expressly designed to bring the whole of human life into the ambit of the sacred."[8]

I was inspired to adopt my children, partially by James 1:27, which says that "pure and genuine religion in the sight of God the Father means caring for orphans and widows in their distress and refusing to let the world corrupt you" (NLT). If that's religion, then sign me up. A religion rooted in relationship with a God whose arms are thrown wide in welcome.

FOR REFLECTION AND DISCUSSION:

Draw a line with "in" written at one end and "out" written at the other. Think of groups of young people, various sub-cultures and tribes, and, thinking of your church / youth work, place them where you think they are on the line.

What are barriers to welcoming those young people who are more "out" than "in"?

7. Dulles, *Models of the Church*, 205.
8. Armstrong, "The myth of religious violence."

10

Value them

Why we need time-rich communities

PRESENTER: "WE WOULD ENCOURAGE you to maximize on the time you have."

Me: "What? make the most of a whole five minutes?

[I rub my hands together, gleefully]

"I can't wait to get started."

I was appalled by the answer. This was a significant youth work conference, and the seminar was packed out. I couldn't fault the passion for youth ministry on display, and there were some excellent ideas being shared. It was half-way through the Q&A when it all went wrong. From the floor I shared where we were at in youth ministry:

"We worked out that although a young person might be involved in our programs for anything from 3 to 10 hours per week, on average we spent 3 minutes in quality time with any one young person per week. What would you do?"

The reply produced a knot in my stomach. "Maximize on the time you have." Bennett has a word for that:

"Junk."

Sure, there were deeper moments with individuals, but if you were the average young person in our youth ministry you got fractionally more than the time it takes to nuke your cold coffee.

Yaconelli took a step back from the front lines of ministry to reflect on the extent to which efforts in youth ministry had taken ground. He realized

VALUE THEM

that, "Discipleship requires a huge investment of time. And most of us don't have the time. Or our current models of ministry don't allow us the time."

He goes on to state most categorically: "Youth ministry as an experiment has failed," but, rather than simply throw out the baby with the bathwater, he points us to reform: "If we want to see the church survive, then we need to rethink youth ministry."[1]

One autumn evening, I had my older-lads group chopping wood for over an hour. Nothing beats youth work when you combine life skills with getting jobs done! Developmentally, it was great. Simeon's demeanor was full of self-doubt, and his first "chop" led to immediate dismissal of his ability and potential. Others rallied around him and, by using slo-mo mode on the iPhone, we were able to identify technique issues in minute detail. 30 minutes later, and the logs were falling apart as he brought down the ax.

And I had a revelation.

The reason we chop wood up for the fire is not just so we can fit the logs in: my fireplace is a good size. It's also to speed up the time it takes to season the wood and create more surface area to be exposed to the fire. Increase the surface area of the exposed wood, and you increase the rate of maturation, and raise the intensity of the fire.

I don't just see Simeon for a handful of minutes on a Sunday, but on Monday and Friday nights as well . . . and I would love to hang out with him more. Jim Collins is right—it's never about the one big event, although that can be a catalyst. It's about the continual engagement that builds momentum.

Maximize on the time you have? No, you need to re-orient the way you do ministry. Mark Oestreicher challenges youth ministries to relocate from "assumptions and values and methods that are outdated for the teenagers we passionately want to serve today,"[2] to a place that builds on the question:

"Where do I belong and who do I relate to?"

He contends that, while youth ministry as we have framed it has centered first on Identity (the question, Who am I?), and then on Autonomy (Why do I exist?), it now needs to move to the third core task of adolescence: Affinity. Oestreicher goes on to suggest that this "has become the pathway to identity formation and autonomy."[3] While I disagree that we have pro-

---

1. Yaconelli, *Getting Fired for the Glory of God*, 109.
2. Oestreicher, *Youth Ministry 3.0*, 43.
3. Oestreicher, *Youth Ministry 3.0*, 70.

gressed from one to the other, being far to reductionist in approach, I do think he gives us food for thought. One definition of the word affinity is to be related "by ties other than blood"[4] - exactly my reading of the church: many members but one body. The body of Christ, by definition, is made up of distinct parts that bear a symbiotic relationship with the others. As mentioned earlier, *one-anothering* consistently trumps leadership (as we know it) in the New Testament vision of the people of God. And these take an investment of time far beyond an hour on Sunday.

THE INCARNATION INCANTATION

A polarisation has emerged between incarnational ministry and programmed ministry, with all of the energy in terms of writing shifting to the relational, with Andy Root and Richard Passmore particularly notable in driving the conversation forward in the US and UK respectively.

Did I say *energy*?

Dean Borgman contends that, "Just as God became the Living Word in human culture, so the Word must today reincarnated or translated in cultural terms."[5] Pimlott explains that the term 'incarnation' is used to describe the way youth workers become Jesus to young people. An incarnational approach, they argue, focuses on relationships and identifying with people, just as Jesus did, being alongside people and engaging in their everyday lives.[6] Leonard Sweet writes that we can attempt to "make Christianity into a religion of excarnation, but you will fail. Christianity is and always has been a religion of incarnation. It puts on flesh and blood, [being] inescapably material, physical and cultural."[7] Borgman sketches out an image of youth ministers "called to waste time with young people."[8] Pete Ward writes that working incarnationally is demanding and difficult, offering no set boundaries, and making youth workers feel vulnerable,[9] yet contends that "the youthworker is a concrete sign of God's interest and presence."[10] Root wrapped up his seminal work on relational ministry, concluding that

4. http://www.dictionary.com/browse/affinity
5. Borgman, *When Kumbaya Is Not Enough*, 7.
6. Pimlott and Pimlott, *Youth Work After Christendom*, 75.
7. Sweet, *Viral*, 28.
8. Borgman, "Youth, Culture, and Media," 13.
9. Ward, *Youthwork and the Mission of God*, 14.
10. Ward, *God at the Mall*, 60.

"the Incarnation is not about influence, but accompaniment,"[11] and even Lawrence asserts ""being with" is another way of saying "incarnational.""[12] The problem is, Jesus didn't just come to *be* with us. His actions were never random acts of kindness, but deliberate, purposeful and clear. Green underscores this, stating that "as Mark 1:38 shows, he even abandons some people whom he had taught so that he could go to teach others [. . .] The normative issue for Jesus was his teaching, his words."[13] Jesus even self-identifies His mission as to "seek and save the lost" (Luke 19:10). We have some work to do.

It "gained prominence in the UK in the 1990s [having been] a mainstay American model since YoungLife introduced it in the 1950s,"[14] but incarnation has become virtual incantation, with a growing belief that something magical happens when we incarnate that cannot be achieved through programmed activity. Actually, the truth is quite the opposite. Magic is formulaic, whereas faith is messy, and rarely follows a prescribed pattern, and obedience to Christ can take you in all sorts of directions (though never outside of God's revealed Word). We have created a false dichotomy between relational and attractional, detached and center-based, and throwing the weight of the Incarnation behind the first seems a *coup de grâce*.

There are significant problems with using the Incarnation of Christ as the basis for incarnational ministry:

1. the Incarnation was a one-off, never-to-be-repeated act. Jesus Christ—the God-man, the Word-made-flesh, our Emmanuel, God with us. "There is a faulty assumption that the incarnation is a model for ministry, such that Christians should imitate the act of the eternal Word becoming incarnate."[15] Borgman rightly pointed out the need for contextualization, yet he makes an unnecessary theological leap from the incarnation, using the "because this, then that" exegetical fallacy.

2. Building a model for ministry from the Incarnation borders on trivializing it. The gulf He bridged was heaven and earth, time and eternity,

---

11. Root, *Revisiting Relational Youth Ministry*, 79.
12. Lawrence, *Jesus Centred Youth Ministry*, 86.
13. Green, "The Incarnation and Mission," 137.
14. Gough, *Rebooted*, 7.
15. Billings, *Union with Christ*, 13-4.

transcendence and immanence. Such can hardly be compared with a missionary moving from the US to Angola, or a youth worker sitting down on a worn park bench to listen to a young person.[16] Root does, however, claim his interpretation of incarnational ministry is not a model lest "it turn into a way of functioning."[17]

3. Jesus didn't actually have to incarnate into Jewish culture—He was born Jewish, and His Father the God of Israel . . . no missionary, then, can ever incarnate as thoroughly into a culture as to be at the level that Jesus was, reaching out to "the lost sheep of Israel" (Matthew 15:24).

4. Jesus' ministry is actually separated from the Incarnation by 30 years, and when it does happen, it's very much a short-term mission, being no more than 3 years. Clearly, this wasn't a pattern to be passed down from generation to generation, as the disciples were called to follow into ministry much earlier.

5. Finally, when put in practice it "essentially illustrates a god-complex, shifted the church from sharing the good news of Jesus to telling others they can just be themselves."[18]

We might, though, create space for the incarnational ministry as "humble, selfless service."[19] Brian Hebblethwaite contends that "the pattern of Christ's self-emptying, his life of service and the way of the cross have determined the characteristic shape of Christian life and action."[20] We can draw from the Incarnation a way of living that puts flesh on the theological bones. This means not simply asking questions about God, but looking to ground it with a response: so what?

Incarnational ministry can be distilled into three ideas: Following the way of Christ, Experiencing the presence of Christ, and Participating in the mission of Christ.

---

16. Ott and Strauss, *Encountering Theology*, 101.
17. Root, 'The Incarnation', *JYM*, 23.
18. Belsterling, *A Defense of Youth Ministry*, 33.
19. Ott and Strauss, *Encountering Theology*, 98-102.
20. Brian Hebblethwaite, "Incarnation," 211.

Value them
Following the way of Christ

Alex, Jeb and Ollie were new to the Christian festival scene and joining 8,000 others in Soul Survivor's Big Top was quite an experience. That particular year the British weather had decided to move indoors, and the floor was soaked by day 2, with a crowd sporting either full rain gear or shorts and flip-flops in a paradoxical reality. On account of a deluge of teenagers, the local town sold out of what Brits refer to as wellies,[21] those essential, and at some point in the mid-noughties, suddenly fashionable boots.

At the end of the service, the young people began to disperse, and I looked around at the carnage left behind—snotty wipes, empty snack containers, drink cartons, clumps of mud, toilet rolls. I turned to the 3 lads.

Me: "Fancy staying behind to help clear this lot up?"

Up for anything, they joined in, and we contributed 7 huge bags of trash to the pile collected by the stewards. As we brought in the final offering, the chief steward, Al, bald and severe-looking, came right up to us. His face broke out into a big grin.

Al: "Thanks, boys. Great job."

For the rest of the night they were buzzing. They were, of course, now on first name terms with the chief steward, and had been personally thanked for their effort. This wasn't sugar-induced but feeling the reward of a great compliment having pulled a shift.

The next night I didn't even need to suggest it. We got on with the business of clearing trash when they could have been at *Mr Boogies*, the funk venue, *Underground* for the urban vibe, or at the sports hall. They chose to serve. In a very real sense, they followed me as I followed Christ (1 Corinthians 11:1).

To top the night off, I noticed Alex scanning the room for Al. Nothing. There was a collective unspoken disappointment as we trudged out of the Big Top, and I realized there was something here for them.

"Wasn't it great when Al came and thanked us? But we didn't do it for the applause."

"God sees the smallest act of love, the hidden service, and loves it."

"He's the only audience I want to please."

In each of those three young men I see servant heartedness. And it happened at a festival where time was created to walk in the footsteps of the Servant-King.

---

21. Gum boots in the US and Canada.

Looking Good Naked

Experiencing the presence of Christ

I'm often surprised where God seems to turn up. The presence of Christ by His Spirit can be experienced everywhere from the after-hours worship session at Soul Survivor to the aftermath of the tragic death of a teenager. The Spirit does not rock up based on an incantation but an invitation, and in my travels, often seemingly regardless of anything we do. That's grace for you.

Christ's presence is guaranteed when we meet together, although ditch the superficial reading of Matthew 18:20, for a deeper one. I've heard the expression "where two or three are gathered" to justify church down the pub. It's not that you can't experience church there, but the choice of Scripture. Jesus speaks those words off the back of difficult teaching about church conflict. You could amplify it like this:

"Even if the darkest moments of conflict with a Christian brother or sister, I am there in the thick of it."

The body is meant to be together, to resist the atomizing nature of our culture that seeks to separate and put in tidy boxes, with Cosby contending that "Far too often youth ministries have become separate enclaves within a church, rather than functioning alongside and becoming an integral element of the body life of the congregation."[22] That must mean going beyond the Sunday service and midweek meeting.

There isn't the space to explore residential work in detail and depth here, but building retreats into programming and the ecclesiological pattern of each year rather than seeing them as bolt-on extras is essential.[23] It is here where we "chop the wood" from the start of the chapter, creating far more opportunity to experience and be the body of Christ, listen to the stories of young people and broaden the horizons of every participant. Whilst youth retreats and festivals facilitate adult-student interaction, if we are able to create spaces for intergenerational gatherings we will move further away from ministry as something *done* to young people, and towards shared ministry experiences.

After 5 days of intense activity and community building in a local park, the young people were desperate for their phones back, a long hot shower, a good meal, and their own beds (in that order!). Two weeks later we received a letter from a non-Christian parent. It was short, but spoke powerfully:

---

22. Cosby, *Giving up Gimmicks*, 28-9.
23. Stapleton, "Residential Disillusion?" 12.

"You have enlarged my son's heart."

Wow. God had been there, more intensely involved than we will ever know. And He is there with you, amid the hive of your activity and relationship work. And it's that presence which brings people back for more.

Each year thousands of people fly to Ibiza, party capital of Europe, to hear the best DJ's in the world drop massive tunes. 24-7 prayer joined the scene at the turn of the millennium, and it now has a drop-in center just off the main strip in the West End, San Antonio.[24] Joining them for a week in the summer, I went out with the interns until 5am, walking the streets and praying.

I met 19-year-old Gaz perched on the side of a water fountain. He seemed to be looking after his friend, who had his head between his knees, sitting in his own vomit, drifting in and out of consciousness.

"How's your buddy doing?"

Within minutes I'm listening as a 19-year-old poured out his heart in a thick Geordie accent. A day before he came out to Ibiza he was carrying the coffin of his Nan. He hadn't grieved, in his words, "staying strong for his dad," and had come to Ibiza to get away from it all, clear his head and have a laugh. The bad news for him was that pain travelled economy too. He said he was an atheist, but when I smiled and asked if I could pray for him, he didn't hesitate. I grabbed his hand and put my other hand on his back and prayed short and sweet, asking Jesus to meet with him in his grief, for the Holy Spirit to work in him so that he might experience the love of the Father.

Me: "Amen."

His friend had returned to consciousness, and Gaz exploded.

Gaz: "You gotta get this guy to pray with you. Make sure you hold his hand at the same time!"

There was nothing magical about the handholding, but this wasn't the time to straighten his theology.

Participating in the on-going story of Christ

Journeying with. Hanging out. Wasting time. Getting alongside. Being there. I'm not sure I have ever read a youth *ministry* text without these concepts reverberating through the pages. They are at the heart of youth work practice and find resonance with Christian concepts of relationship. Bright

---

24. Check out their ministry at http://www.24-7ibiza.com/

and Bailey go as far as contending that, "'being there' is the theological outworking of being like Jesus."[25] Hmm. It might be *part* of it, but if that's true, we have just reduced the good news of Jesus to playing dodgeball. There must be an imperative—young people do not need a 28-year-old best friend! The danger also exists that "Christian youth workers can become so effective at relating to 'non-Christian' young people that [their] beliefs are validated rather than challenged."[26]

"Preach the Gospel at all times, and if necessary, use words."

Nice strap-line, bad theology, and it's unlikely St Francis of Assisi ever uttered it. To reduce the incarnation to hanging out with young people is to miss out on what Jesus did, and therefore, what we as His body are to do. Tina, one of our volunteers, was desperate for others to see the difference her faith made but didn't want to be *preachy* at the school gate. One afternoon, it happened. Lisa lingered around while other parents took their children home.

Lisa: "I've wanted to ask for so long. There's something different about you. Do you do Reiki?"

Tina went from super-pumped to deflated in about 2 seconds. There are limitations of being with: "Jesus did not come into the world to 'be with' people; he came to teach them."[27] His actions were backed up by words, and words with actions. Jesus did a lot of stuff but also said a lot of stuff too. To participate means to get stuck in, continuing the story when Acts 28 leaves off.

THE BALANCING ACT

Returning to our reflection on incarnational ministry, Steve Griffiths offers a powerful critique of what he sees as "theological and ministerial laziness,"[28] notably on the part of trainers. He writes that,

> "Contrary to popular opinion, the truth is that Jesus did not 'hang out' with people. Jesus did not wait to 'earn the right' before embarking on the kerygmatic imperative. Indeed, the very opposite is true. His earthly ministry lasted only two or three years. In that time, he constantly wandered the countryside, towns and cities of

25. Bright, *Youth Work*, 151.
26. Jolly, in Smith, Stanton, and Wylie, *Youth Work and Faith*, 28.
27. Green, "The Incarnation and Mission," 136.
28. Griffiths, *Models for Youth Ministry*, 5.

Value them

Israel, never staying in one place long enough to build relationships with those he met. It may not be an exaggeration to state that, in reality, Jesus had a 'hit and run' ministry."[29]

He is so right. Yes, Jesus clothed Himself in flesh, as only a human could be the perfect sacrifice for the remission of sins, but he moved from town to town, village to village, teaching and ministering, doing what Griffiths calls *hit and run* ministry. Even with His closest, it's unlikely that Jesus spent more than two years out of the three in intensive discipleship.

That said, ever journeyed with a young person from 12 to 14, or 15 to 17? Two years is a seriously long time for a teenager! Sitting in my office for interview, Matthew looked the part in his tie and jacket. He reflected on how he had been in such a bad place with God when he was younger, but he was ready now for Bible College. I pushed a little more. He was talking about events that happened in the same calendar year as we were meeting! Wow. Incarnational ministry, as understood as *humble, selfless service*, demands that we are time-rich in both quality AND quantity. This kind of understanding of incarnational ministry is pivotal to our expression as the Body of Christ.

What does that mean? Here's the headline: programmed ministries can embody what many articulate as incarnational ministry just as effectively as detached, relational work. There is a place for big, programmed youth work and ministry, as these not only provide opportunity for experiencing the presence of Christ and participation in His story, but also open the door for deeper relationships. Belsterling asserts that, "the Church desperately needs youth ministries that are specifically focused on building intentionally influential relationships between adults and teenagers."[30] Programming can act as a time-rich vehicle for connecting, and attempts to create a false dichotomy between relational and programming only serves to undermine great youth work, and distract youth workers from the task.

---

29. Griffiths, *Models for Youth Ministry*, 5.
30. Belsterling, *A Defense of Youth Ministry*, 7.

11

Hitting the city streets
How to be confident about church

DOES IT TAKE A whole church to raise a child? Krish Kandiah, at the time working for the Evangelical Alliance, certainly thought so suggesting that "youth ministry is simply too big a job to be left to us youth workers."[1] The stats back him up. While in 2010 some 375,300 under 15s attended church, in 2020 that figure drops to 183,700. Peter Brierley's research was highlighted by Scripture Union who have been refocussing their work on the massive 95% of children and young people who do not access church.[2] We need work rooted in families and not isolated from the communities that young people live within—a place where parents are allies and team mates rather than enemies.[3] Youth workers, as Rob Parsons points out, are not solely responsible for the spiritual nurture of young people in a church setting whatever their JD might suggest.[4]

I agree with Kandiah . . . although I don't think that he goes far enough. Individual heroics are a drop in the ocean, and while every drop counts, the cultural tide has swept many young people away from Christian faith. In fact, it has systematically and incrementally widened the generation gap. In

---

1. Kandiah, "It takes a whole church to raise a child," 15.
2. Scripture Union, "The 95 Campaign," https://content.scriptureunion.org.uk/95-campaign
3. Fields, *Your first 2 years*, 103-25.
4. Parsons, "Parents: Sharing the Load," 18-20.

an astounding summary of the impact of historical social forces on young people, David White notes how:

1. "Youth were abstracted from *significant social roles* in communities. (Youth roles are now limited to education, consumption, peer relationships.)
2. Youth were abstracted from *networks of care* in communities. (Youth are largely relegated to peer relationships with little adult involvement.)
3. Youth were abstracted from *attention to the common good*. (Youth today are seduced by marketers to focus upon commodities and sumptuous lifestyles.)
4. Youth were abstracted from *families and other local authorities*. (Youth are relegated primarily to peer groups.)
5. Youth were abstracted from innate *"passions and sensibilities,"* described by Stanley G. Hall as intellectual curiosity, compassion, passion for life, beauty and justice. (many youth experience curiosity and passion as unnecessary and irrelevant for vocational advancement.)
6. Youth were abstracted from *expectation to fully attend to the call of God* upon their lives. (For many youth, the need for security and desire for consumption drives lifestyle and vocational choices.)
7. Youth were abstracted from *faith communities*. (Youth are relegated to special but marginal status as adolescents.)
8. Youth were abstracted from *their own powers as agents of God in history*, shaping a better world. (Schools and other social roles do not expect or challenge youth to explore their own powers and abilities.)"[5]

The truth is it takes a society to raise a child, and we have infantilized and objectified them. Yet as we have been working through this text we can see how the recovery of a robust ecclesiology begins to dismantle the abstractions one by one. It takes more than just programming, although don't make that the enemy. If our Christian communities stop sometime after 1pm on Sunday until 10am 7 days later, with perhaps two or three hours on a week day evening, can we really expect the young people in those communities to live out the values for the other 162 hours of the week?

Our failure has been the lack of prioritisation of faith transmission, and the current push towards all things mentoring and discipleship feel

5. White, "The Social Construction of Adolescence," 18-9.

like last-ditch efforts to hang on to what remains. But it feels like too little too late. Results from the 2011 UK church survey revealed a fascinating truth. Rather than a generation losing its faith, each new generation is less religious than its predecessor, articulated by the headline that, "change is between, not within generations."[6]

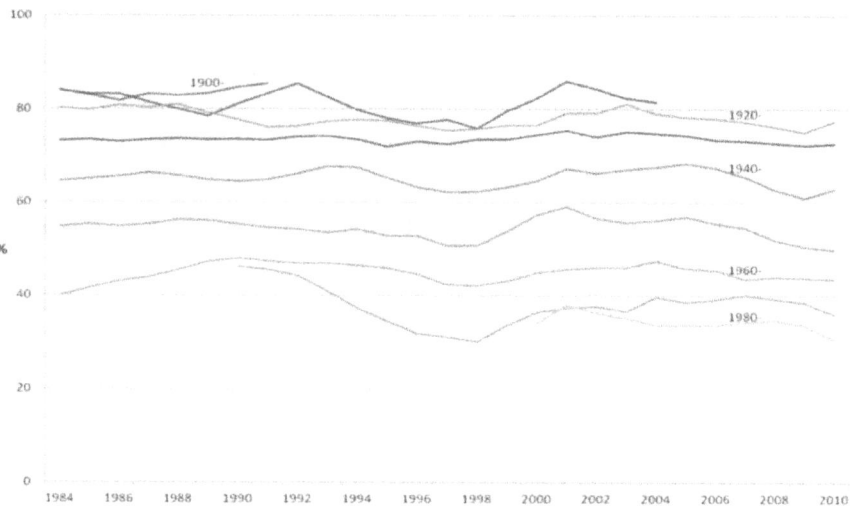

Figure 22: Religious Affiliation by Decade of Birth, 1981-2011[7]

Between 2005 and 2015 UK church attendance for those under 30 dropped by a quarter[8] and given that older Christians in general belonged to churches as young people, this is what Walker calls a ticking "time bomb" for the traditional denominations in particular.[9] Statistics can be manipulated and argued over, but I do not want to wait around to see if the next 3 or 4 lines on the graph will take us further towards ground zero. So what is it going to cost? First, a rejection of easy answers and *blag it and grab it* solutions. It takes more than breaking down the age barriers within our worship services and reducing the sense of young people being second class, ushered out of the main auditorium to their own, age-appropriate sessions. What good is a vote in church over the color of the paint when

6. Voas and Watt, *Numerical change in church attendance*, 10.
7. British Social Attitudes Survey, 1983-2011 (excludes non-white respondents).
8. Brierley, *UK Church Statistics 2005-2015*.
9. Walker, *Testing Fresh Expressions*, 7, 42.

central government refuses to allow teens to shape policy through political influence?

It takes more than increasing the number of adults involved in discipling young people; more than superhero grit and determination from twenty-something role models; more than supporting and resourcing parents and carers to nurture more effectively; more than involving young people in the main worship band or speaking from the front. It takes a compelling vision for life, a set of values that foster virtues and which permeate a culture, and the opportunities for that vision to be achieved.

If we cannot effectively empower and release the young people to live as authentic Christians in their daily-lived reality in the time we have with them, we need to radically rethink our approach. The cultural tide is simply too strong to go it alone. It's easy to suggest that churches should be like life-boats, pulling in those who are drowning, rescuing them from the malevolent waters. Great idea, but the capacity is always smaller than needed, and used as a defensive, reactionary and protectionist strategy. Rather, our approach must be to permeate the culture, "wearing clothes like costumes, always to celebrate and communicate, never to hide,"[10] as Pete Greig puts it. Every Christian is an advocate for the kingdom of God, playing their part. The body, working effectively, is designed to do something more than just self-care. It is designed to attract, just like the perfect body images presented to us in perfume and shaving adverts, chiseled figures subconsciously telling us what we should aspire to be like.

Imagine for a moment.

What would the church look like at *its best*?

Is it a compelling picture to you? If not, let me try to sketch it out a little. Where the former UK Prime Minister, David Cameron's Big Society vision had appeal to releasing grass-roots initiatives but literally no resources to make it stick, the church excels. I see a body that people known not for what it stands against, but what it stands for. Not for the grand architecture or state of the art, fully digital audio-visual department, but for the lives that are transformed by the gospel. Not for rejecting the last, least and lost, but for welcoming the broken, providing families for the forgotten, and embracing the "sinners".

So let's start at home.

---

10. Greig, *The Vision and the Vow*.

A QUICK RECAP

In this book we have sought to develop an ecclesiology for youth work for this exact task of ushering in the kingdom of God through personal and community transformation. Without a clear theology of work with young people, and not wanting to overstretch theological ideas around the incarnation, or simply go with the pragmatic, the church provides an obvious and compelling location for reflection. This is not least because the church is the biggest employer of youth workers, has the largest number of volunteers, and works with more young people each week than any other organisation!

Yet all too often the tenure of a youth worker at a church does not endure. UK Christian youth work thinker, James Ballantyne, suggests this is down to four primary reasons:

1. Risk-averse churches
2. Bad management
3. Parachurch drift
4. Burn out[11]

The body of Christ metaphor is the swiss army knife of the church, with a flexibility and breadth that other images and theological constructs just cannot match. Yet unlike my friend's use of the multi-tool to describe me in chapter 3, the body of Christ adds both range and potency to the various tools. In chapter 2 we considered the need for definition in both the job description and the person specification, even if that is not a formal contract, and you are doing this as an extra-timer. Chapter 3 went further into who we are and the baggage we bring to the table, suggesting that, as people of the Bible who belong to each other through the body of Christ, we get back to the theological underpinning of who we are and why we do what we do. With the use of the Johari Window in the Action Points, the scene was set for Chapter 4's approach to starting out with what little you might have. There is plenty of material for continuing to build effective work, in particular the need for the breath of God through our ministries, and growth through loss. Chapter 5 reviewed the limits to the shepherding image often operant in ministry, and set out the recruitment strategy for the all-star game that is more consistent with the "one-anothering" of the

---

11. Ballantyne, "These 4 Reasons".

body of Christ than the call and commissioning of King Saul, noted by 1 Samuel 9:2 as not only "handsome", but also "without equal" (BSB) and "head and shoulders taller than anyone else in the land" (NLT).

Chapter 6 took this further, with a more in-depth look at every member ministry. This opened up two related ideas: First, the impact of Christ as our commander-in-chief on the notion of leadership within the body. Second, how a great body image pushes against the Western cultural agenda of autonomy and individualization that has bred record levels of loneliness, social isolation and immaturity. In many ways, the hard work was done at this point, with chapters 7 through 10 finding resonance within the body of Christ for the four core values of youth work. Although shorter than the other chapters, these added wider perspectives of body language that would not have been seen otherwise: the nature of our relationship to one another through the work of the Spirit; the limits to empowerment; the need for removing barriers that takes seriously the tensions of a superficial equality agenda; and a richer theological platform for relational ministry. It's been an intense journey. My hope is that this small contribution pushes against the drift away from the church that Ballantyne outlines.

His third concern, the drift away from working with young people through a church to doing so through parachurch resonates, having worked in both settings. Yes, youth work and ministry has often been compelled to move to the margins when church has not—just look at the work of Frontier Youth Trust who sought to find *StreetSpace* for the presence of God, and the many others who have adopted an Outside-in or Outside-out approach. Can the body of Christ hold work with both churched and unchurched in tension? Kageler writes, "I'm not saying we need to automatically bail out of church-based youth ministry if we have a heart for the lost. I am saying integrity demands that we bail if we have no heart for the found."[12] I believe that the local expression of church is the hope for our world, and, armed with a compelling body image, the gospel can go viral.

REBORN YOUTH WORK

In his book, *Rebooted*, Tim Gough works through the genres of scripture using the framework noted in Chapter 3, working through the *critical task* of asking what the bible says about young people (putting our own cultural baggage and contemporary reading to one side), before engaging with

---

12. Kageler, in Devries, *Sustainable*, 235.

the *constructive task*, asking how this biblical exposition can inform our practice today. By working through a selected reading of Scripture, he built towards a biblical framework for youth work, which is presented in the form of 8 principles, held together by what he defines as the youth work facilitator (see figure 23). I am not the biggest fan of acrostics, but Gough's model is definitely rich in content.

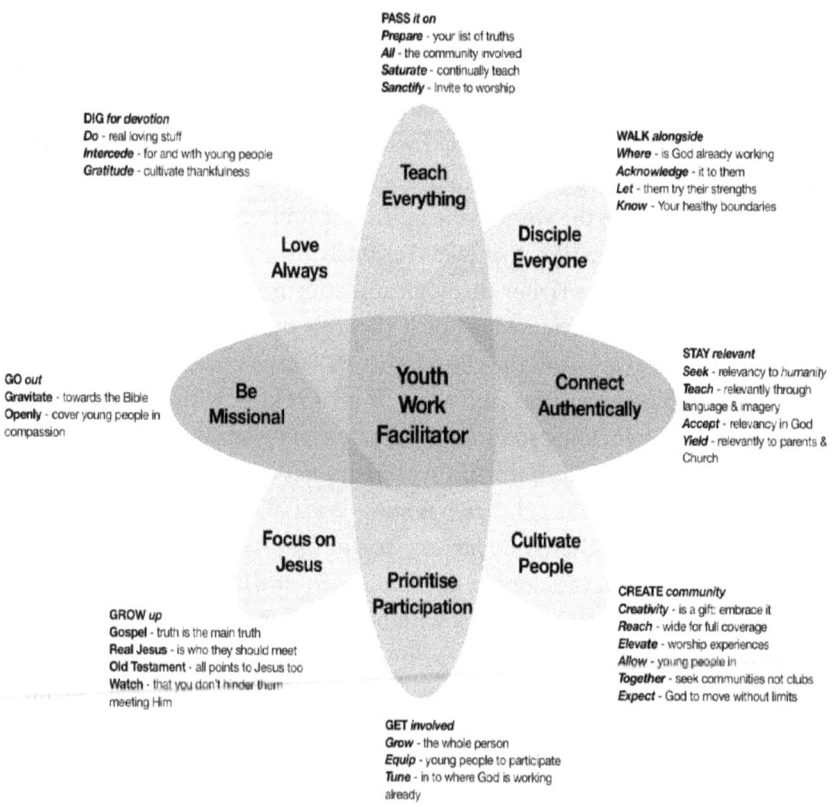

Figure 23: Gough's Biblical Model for Youth Work[13]

The youth pastor and youth worker simply cannot do all of these by themselves, and neither should they. There is only one who is omni-gifted, and that same Spirit works his gifts through the members of the body (1 Corinthians 12:4-11). In fact, these 8 principles reflect everything that I would

13. Gough, *Rebooted*, 171, used by permission.

suggest is a healthy body image from chapter 6, with young people joining with adults, empowered in their giftings to contribute—a far cry from the experience in many churches. Kinnaman pushes against the normative cultural separation contending, "rather than being defined by segregated age groups, however practical they seem [. . .] we are called to connect our past with our future." Drawing on the imagery of the heavenly city in Hebrews 12:22-4, he continues, "Intergenerational relationships matter because they are a snapshot of Zion, a small but true picture of the majesty and diversity of God's people throughout the ages [. . .] a living, breathing body of Christ."[14] In this sense, "The church is supposed to be a sociological miracle - a demonstration that Jesus has died and risen to create a new humanity composed of all sorts of people."[15]

There is a deeper truth here concerning the relationship of young people within the body. The failing at the top of the ladder of participation model is that it puts the focus on the relationship of the young people to the adults concerned. The ultimate empowerment isn't that young people initiate the decision making, but that the boundary between adult and young person is removed—the sociological distinctions reduced in the light of the theological imperative of body language. The highest rung of the ladder is seen when it genuinely doesn't matter who initiates the decision. Young people are seen as part of the body, and all parts are encouraged to contribute. Gough concludes that,

> "A superstar youth pastor is often left to be the sole teacher, discipler, and evangelist of young people - something we don't find in the pages of the Bible; whereas a facilitator understands how to marshal a much broader collection of resources to that end. Please, be a pastor, but even more, be a facilitator. Help ministry happen! Develop people, teams, the church, and young people all towards the goal of growing healthy youth ministry."[16]

Like I said earlier, leaders are ligaments. So does this spell the end of the superhero youth minister? Let me share a story with you.

One Sunday I was on the loading team for our church, and the ministry intern asked me if I ever stopped. Its not that I set time trials for every event in my life, but I like to work hard and fast. And if I can get a PB (personal best), then all the better. Some of you will relate to the activist in me.

---

14. Kinnaman, *You Lost Me*, 204.
15. Drew, *A Journey Worth Taking*.
16. Gough, *Rebooted*, 172.

Are there dangers? Yes. When I was 18, I worked for the wine and spirits distributor for a large groceries chain. My job was simple: Look at the list, jump on a pallet truck (like a mini-fork lift, without the cab and with minimal lift capability!), locate the pallets stacked with boxes of alcohol, and drive them on to the trailers so the drivers could keep the stores stocked. One particular morning, the pressure was on. A truck had got caught up in standstill traffic and the floor manager pulled us off other jobs to get this one done as quickly as humanly possible. He set about directing the rig into the bay while a fleet of pallet trucks set off across the warehouse. I led the charge, slamming my ride into the first wine mountain, activating the lift mech, and driving it out, load-forward, towards the trailer. I leant left and right to check for obstacles in my path, as my direct sight was blocked by boxes stacked 8 high. I lined myself up nicely and hit the steel ramp at speed, so I could get in and out before the next driver came in. Then it happened. I suddenly realized that I had stopped moving forwards. The motor driving the small wheels pitched higher than a dog whistle, as they were no longer touching the surface. My pallet truck, loaded with several thousand pounds worth of alcohol, teetered over the edge of the ramp. The manager, in his frantic activity, hadn't put the loading flap out properly. Time stopped. Everything seemed perfectly balanced. All except me. I bailed with a 12-foot leap from the controls. And then gravity took over. The pallet, in slo-mo, began to tip, irreversibly, downwards. Every single bottle shattered, and a sea of red wine washed the shop floor. I stood in stunned silence as everything in the warehouse came to an abrupt stop. People must have woken up with a hangover the next morning, such was the overwhelming aroma of wine.

In the beatitudes, Jesus never said, "Blessed are the balanced, for they shall never spill a drop." Jesus sent the scales scattering across the temple floor, then spilt His precious blood in the most extreme sport the Romans possessed: Crucifixion. We have become obsessed with balance, whether work-life, diets, education, exercise . . . Even our theology. We have a badge to describe that kind of person: *Sound*. We've bought into the cult of happy medium and sanitized the gospel, making *balance* the 10th fruit of the Spirit. Stop googling how to remove the metaphorical blood stains from the Christian faith and running round with wet wipes! Indeed, "Youth ministry seeking lasting changes must flow out of the theology of the cross."[17] Rebooted? I think reborn is more in sync with the continuing ministry of

---

17. Cole and Nielson, *Gospel-Centered Youth Ministry*, 30.

Christ through the Spirit. Very simply, "Gospel centred youth workers operate out of a biblical theology that understands Jesus as the fulfilment of salvation history (Luke 24:27; Galatians 3:8), and then calls students to repent of their sin because of the gracious love of God that is theirs by faith in Christ Jesus."[18] It's not the sexiest premise, but then again we set out in this book to not just dress down, but to throw out our fast fashion wardrobes, and as the body of Christ to walk out naked, confident in our self image.

1 Peter 2:21 tells us that "Christ suffered for us, leaving an example, that we should follow in His steps." Being a church full of Jesus followers means walking, running, jumping into the same messy places that He did. Being faith-full to Jesus will lead you away from the beaten path. It will mean stepping out at times when everyone around says this doesn't make sense. Yaconelli even suggested that "if those called to youth ministry follow the lead of the One who called them, then getting fired is inevitable."[19]

If you think that the 10% will satisfy God, or that regular attendance at church is enough, or your youth ministry involvement ticks the box for Christian service, you are misinformed about what following Jesus is about.

Christ as the head calls His body towards extreme acts, yet we play it safe. Let's get back to our book, and back to our man, the Lord Jesus Christ, and walk as He walked, do as He did, bringing light, life and love into a world seemingly bent on self-destruction. Silence the body-shamers in media and the political arena by strutting our stuff in the world around us through proclamation of the good news. Let's be louder yet kinder in our approach, confident that Jesus will build his *ekklesia* and the gates of hell will not overcome it (Matthew 16:18).

God has one plan: the Body of Christ, but don't make this about balance. Part of being the body is to connect the extremities to each other and making the most of them, rather than leave them untethered. Systems that work together for good, just like hand-eye co-ordination, that release, bless and minister God's love to the world. To take the good news of Jesus Christ to places that desperately need it, from the rural parishes of Buckinghamshire to the Favelas of Brazil. From the city lights of Tokyo to war-torn nations like Syria. From the suburbs of California to the migrants camping in Calais. This is a shout out to all those disaffected heroes going it alone: don't give up on the body. It connects the hands and feet of Jesus. To those who keep swinging one foot in front of the other in church-based ministry: keep

18. McGarry, *A Biblical Theology*, 116.
19. Yaconelli, *Getting Fired*, 95.

holding on to that vision. Keep it front-loaded and fresh. Mark Matlock, the Executive Director of Youth Specialties, captures the mature vision well:

> "Youth ministry reminds the church that teens are not marginalized members of the body, but co-creators and conspirators in the divine work of the church, restoring life on earth as it is in heaven."[20]

I could almost end there—If someone has said it better, steal their line and go out on a high. But the point is that it all starts again when you put this book down. It's like looking at yourself in the mirror. It's not there to live your life out in front of it. You've got to turn and walk away. When you do, don't lose sight of what you saw in it—the glorious image of Christ and His body. Such are those who listen to the Word and do not do what it says. "But whoever looks intently into the perfect law that gives freedom and continues in it [even when they step away]—not forgetting what they have heard, but doing it—they will be blessed in what they do." (James 1:23-25).

20. Mark Matlock, "5 Reasons."

Appendix 1
At what age in the UK?

THE FOLLOWING FACTS PROVIDE a snapshot of the restrictions placed on young people in 2020. Adolescence has been extended and there are clear anomalies, such as the ability to join the army and die for your country, yet not be able to order an alcoholic drink, no matter how weak, at a pub.

At 10 years old . . . you can be charged with a crime.

At 12 years old . . . you can take part in performances that are considered dangerous.

At 13 years old . . . you can get a part time job doing 'light work' but this is limited (think "paper round").

At 14 years old . . . you can work for two hours on a school day, between 7 and 8am and 5 and 7pm, plus Saturdays, although this is relaxed during school holidays.

You can order soft drinks in a bar.

If convicted of a criminal offence in a Youth Court, you can be held for no more than 24 months. You could also get a fine for a maximum of £1,000.

Wearing a seatbelt is considered your own personal responsibility.

At 15 years old . . . you can be sent to a young offenders institute for up to two years, on conviction.

At 16 years old . . . you can choose your own doctor, and have the right to give consent to medical, dental, contraceptive and surgical treatment.

You can have sex, gay or straight, so long as your partner is also 16+.

Appendix 1 — At what age in the UK?

You can drink a beer, wine, or cider with a meal in licensed premises if accompanied by an adult.

You can claim benefits, obtain a National Insurance number, and order a passport.

You can ride a moped (maximum 50cc and with a provisional licence), and a ride-on mower!

You can work at the market, join the armed forces, or even get married (with parental consent).

You can move out of the family home with your parents' permission and rent accommodation (a guarantor is required until you're 18).

You can play the National Lottery and buy premium bonds.

If you're 17 and under, it is an offence for someone in a position of trust who is 18 or over to engage in **any kind** of sexual activity with you.

At 17 years old . . . you can drive cars (with a provisional licence and a qualified driver who is at least 21 in the passenger seat, or if you pass the tests, by yourself).

You can apply for a private pilot's licence and fly.

You can be interviewed by the police without an adult present.

You can become a blood donor and leave your body for medical study.

At 18 years old . . . you can vote in local and general elections, and stand for election as a local councillor, Member of Parliament, or even Mayor.

You can serve on a jury, be tried in a magistrate's court and go to jail if found guilty.

If adopted, you can see your original birth certificate.

You can get married without parental permission and make a will.

You can buy fireworks, bladed items, cigarettes and alcohol, bet in a bookies or casino, and get a tattoo.

At 19 years old . . . you are no longer entitled to free full-time education at school.

At 21 years old . . . you can apply to adopt a child, and supervise a learner driver (as long as you've held a driving licence for three years).

Appendix 2
David's Mighty Men (the Gibborim)

Key texts: **2 Samuel 23:8-39, 1 Chronicles 11:10-47**

Where did they come from? All over Israel. *"So David left Gath and escaped to the cave of Adullam. Soon his brothers (!!) and all his other relatives joined him there. Then others began coming – men who were in trouble or in debt or who were just discontented – until David was the captain of about 400 men."* 1 Samuel 22:1-2

THE THREE

"Lord forbid I should drink! This water is as precious as the blood of these men who risked their lives to bring me a drink." 2 Samuel 23:17			
Josheb-Basshebeth aka Jashobeam	the Tahkemonite (possibly Ishbaal, Saul's son. The editor may downplay heroics)	The leader	Killed 800 men in one encounter with a spear. 2 Samuel 23:8
Eleazar ben Dodai	the Ahohite	Second in command	Stood his ground with David when all else fled, killing until he could no longer carry the sword. 2 Samuel 23:9
Shammah ben Agee	the Hararite		Held back the Philistines, defending a lentil field when the Israelite army fled. 2 Samuel 23:11-12

Appendix 2 — David's Mighty Men (the Gibborim)

THE THIRTY

2 Samuel 23:8-39 & 1 Chronicles 11:10-47	
Name	Alias and further info
Shammah the Harodite	Shammoth
Abishai ahi Joab ben Zeruiah	The leader of the Thirty. Killed 300 in a battle.
Benaiah ben Jehoiada	A valiant warrior. Killed champion fighters, & a lion. Captain of David's bodyguard. Most honoured of the Thirty.
Asahel ahi Joab	
Elhanan ben Dodo	of Bethlehem
Helez the Paltite	
Ira ben Ikkesh	of Tekoa
Abiezer	of Anathoth
Mebunnai the Hushathite	Sibbekai
Zalmon the Ahohite	Ilai
Mahari the Netophathite	
Heleb ben Baanah the Netophathite	Heled
Ithai ben Ribai	of Gibeah of Benjamin
Benaiah the Pirathonite	
Hiddai	of the Ravines of Gaash (Hurai)
Abi-Albon the Arbathite	Abiel
Azmaveth the Barhumite	
Eliahba the Shaalbonite	
the sons of Jashen	sons of Hashem the Gizonite
Jonathan ben Shammah the Hararite	ben Shagee
Ahiam ben Sharar the Hararite	ben Sakar
Eliphelet ben Ahasbai the Maakathite	ben Ur
Hezro the Carmelite	
Paarai the Arbite	Naarai ben Ezbai
Igal ben Nathan	of Zobah (Joel ahi Nathan)
the son of Haggadi	Mibhar ben Hagri
Zelek the Ammonite	
Naharai the Beerothite	the Berothite
Ira the Ithrite	
Gareb the Ithrite	

Appendix 2 — David's Mighty Men (the Gibborim)

2 Samuel 23:8–39 & 1 Chronicles 11:10–47	
Uriah the Hittite	The one and only. 2 Sam 11 Fiercely loyal & honourable

2 Samuel 23:8–39	
Names	
Elika the Harodite	Eliam ben Ahithophel the Gilonite

1 Chronicles 11:10–47	
Names	
Hepher the Mekerathite	Jedieael ben Shimri
Ahijah the Pelonite	Joha the Tizite
Zabad ben Ahlai	Eliel the Mahavite
Adina ben Shiza the Reubenite	Jeribai ben Elnaam
Hanan ben Maakah	Joshaviah ben Elnaam
Joshaphat the Mithnite	Ithma the Moabite
Uzzia the Ashterathite	Eliel
Shama ben Hotham the Aroerite	Obed
Jeiel ben Hotham the Aroerite	Jaasiel the Mezobaite

Bibliography

Aiken, Nick. *Working with Teenagers*. London: HarperCollins, 1994.
All-Party Parliamentary Group on Youth Affairs. *Youth Work Inquiry: Final Report*. April 2019.
Allen, Joseph, and Claudia Worrell Allen. *Escaping the Endless Adolescence*. New York: Ballantine, 2009.
Armstrong, Karen. "The Myth of Religious Violence." *The Guardian,* 25th September 2014, http://www.theguardian.com/world/2014/sep/25/-sp-karen-armstrong-religious-violence-myth-secular.
Arnett, Jeffrey Jensen. *Emerging Adulthood*. New York: Oxford University Press, 2004.
Arzola, Fernando. "The Ecclesial View of Youth Ministry." In *Youth Ministry in the 21st Century: Five Views*. Edited by Chap Clark, 113-23. Grand Rapids: Baker, 2015.
The Avengers. Directed by Joss Whedon. Burbank: Marvel Studios, 2012.
Ballantyne, James. "These 4 Reasons are why Youth Workers are Leaving the Church". *Christianity Today*, 3 October 2017. https://www.christiantoday.com/article/these-4-reasons-are-why-youth-workers-are-leaving-the-church/115209.htm.
Balswick, Judith, and Jack Balswick. *Relationship-Empowerment Parenting*, Grand Rapids: Baker, 2003.
Banks, Robert. *Paul's Idea of Community*. Exeter: Paternoster, 1980.
Batsleer, Janet, and Bernard Davis, eds. *What is Youth Work?* Exeter: Learning Matters, 2010.
Batsleer, Janet, James Duggan, Sarah McNicol, Simone Spray and Kurtis Angel. *Loneliness Connects Us*. Manchester Metropolitan University, 2018.
Belbin, Meredith. *Management Teams: Why they Succeed or Fail*. 3rd Ed. Oxford: Butterworth-Heinemann, 2010.
Belsterling, Ron. *A Defense of Youth Ministry: Attachment Relationship Ministry*. Eugene: Wipf & Stock, 2019.
Bennett, Colin. "Working with Families." In *Christian Youth Work in Theory and Practice*. Edited by Nash, Sally, and Jo Whitehead. 210-222. London: SCM, 2014.
Berard, John, James Penner and Rick Bartlett. *Consuming Youth: Leading Teens through Consumer Culture*. Grand Rapids: Zondervan, 2010.
Billings, J. Todd. *Union with Christ: Reframing Theology and Ministry for the Church*. Grand Rapids: Baker Academic, 2011.
Blenkinsopp, Joseph. *Interpretation, A Bible Commentary for Teaching and Preaching: Ezekiel*. Louisville: John Knox, 1990.

Bibliography

Bock, Daryll. "Why Miracles," *IVP New Testament Commentaries: Luke*. http://www.biblegateway.com/resources/ivp-nt/Why-Miracles.

Bolman, L.G. and T.E. Deal. *Leading with the Soul*. San Francisco: Jossey Bass, 2001.

Bonner, Steven "Understanding the Changing Adolescent." In *Adoptive Youth Ministry: Integrating Emerging Generations into the Family of Faith*, edited by Chap Clark, 22-38. Grand Rapids: Baker Academic, 2016.

Borgman, Dean. *When Kumbaya Is Not Enough: A Practical Theology for Youth Ministry*. Peabody: Hendrickson Publishers, 1997.

———. "Youth, Culture, and Media: Contemporary Youth Ministry." *Transformation* 11 (1994) 13-6.

Brewster, Dan, and Patrick McDonald. *Children – The Great Omission*. Viva Network, 2004.

Brierley, Danny. *Joined Up: An Introduction to Youthwork and Ministry*. Carlisle: Authentic Lifestyle, 2003.

Brierley, Peter. "Where is the Church Going?" *Brierley Consultancy*. http://brierleyconsultancy.com/images/csintro.pdf.

———. *UK Church Statistics 2005-2015*. Tonbridge: ADBC, 2011.

———. *UK Church Statistics No.3 2018*. Tonbridge: ADBC, 2018.

Bright, Graham, ed. *Youth Work: Histories, Policy and Contexts*. London: Palgrave, 2015.

Bruce, F. F. *The Epistle to the Galatians: A Commentary on the Greek Text*. Grand Rapids: Eerdmans, 1982.

Brueggemann, Walter. "Rethinking Church Models Through Scripture" *Theology Today* 48: 2 (1991) 128-38.

Chapman, Alan. "Johari Window Model and Free Diagram." *Businessballs*. 2004. https://www.businessballs.com/self-awareness/johari-window-model-and-free-diagrams/

Clark, Chap. *Adoptive Youth Ministry: Integrating Emerging Generations into the Family of Faith*. Grand Rapids: Baker Academic, 2016.

Clark, Chap, Fernando Arzola, Brian Cosby, Ron Hunter and Greg Stier. *Youth Ministry in the 21st Century: Five Views*. Grand Rapids: Baker, 2015.

Coggin, Stewart. Total Football, n.d., *About.com*. http://worldsoccer.about.com/od/soccercultur1/a/Total-Football.htm.

Cole, Cameron, and Jon Nielson, eds. *Gospel-Centered Youth Ministry: A Practical Guide*. United States: Crossway Books, 2016.

Collins, Jim. *Good to Great*. London: Random House, 2001.

Cosby, Brian H. *Giving Up Gimmicks: Reclaiming Youth Ministry from an Entertainment Culture*. Phillipsburg: P&R, 2012.

Covey, Stephen R. *The 8th Habit: From Effectiveness to Greatness*. New York: Free, 2005.

Creasy Dean, Kenda. *OMG: A Youth Ministry Handbook*. Nashville: Abingdon, 2010.

Creasy Dean, Kenda, Chap Clark and Dave Rahn. *Starting Right*. Grand Rapids: Zondervan, 2001.

Crocodile Dundee. Directed by Peter Fairman. New South Wales: Rimfire Films, 1986.

Davies, Bernard. *Austerity, Youth Policy and the Deconstruction of the Youth Service in England*. London: Palgrave Macmillan, 2019.

Devries, Mark. *Sustainable Youth Ministry*. Downers Grove: IVP, 2008.

Drew, Charles D. *A Journey Worth Taking: Finding Your Purpose in This World*. Phillipsburg: P&R, 2007.

du Feu, Andy. "Making room at the table: A response to Clyne's 'Uncovering Youth Ministry's

Bibliography

Professional Narrative' in Y&P 2015." *Youth & Policy*, (2018) n.p.
Duguid, Iain M. *The NIV Application Commentary: Ezekiel*. Grand Rapids: Zondervan, 1999.
Dulles, Avery. *Models of the Church*. Expanded edition. New York: Doubleday, 1987.
Dunn, James D.G. *The Theology of Paul the Apostle*. Rev. Edition. London: Eerdmans, 2003.
Ecksmanfan, "Editorial: Is Batman a Superhero?" *ComicBookMovie.com*, 3rd February 2012, http://www.comicbookmovie.com/fansites/geekboymovienews/news/?a=55671.
Emery White, James. *What They Didn't Teach You in Seminary*. Grand Rapids: Baker, 2011.
Emery-White, Steve, and Ed Mackenzie. *Networks for Faith Formation: Relational Bonds and the Spiritual Growth of Youth*. Eugene: Wipf and Stock, 2017.
Eastman, Michael. *Outside In*. Falcon Books, 1976.
Ellingworth, Paul. *The Epistle to the Hebrews: A Commentary on the Greek Text*. NIGTC. Carlisle: Paternoster, 1993.
Erickson, Millard J. *Christian Theology*. Grand Rapids: Baker, 1985.
Fee, Gordon D. *The First Epistle to the Corinthians*. Grand Rapids: Eerdmans, 1987.
Fee, Gordon D., and Douglas Stuart. *How to Read the Bible for All Its Worth*. 2nd Edition. Bletchley: Scripture Union, 1993.
Fields, Doug. *Your First Two Years in Youth Ministry*. Grand Rapids: Zondervan, 2002.
Fletcher, Adam. "Ladder of Young People's Participation." *Freechild.org*. http://freechild.org/ladder.htm 2008.
Frozen. Directed by Chris Buck and Jennifer Lee. Burbank: Walt Disney Pictures, 2013.
Gerber, Michael. *The E-Myth Revisited*. London: Harper Collins, 1995.
Gilchrist, Ruth, and Tony Jeffs. *Settlements, Social Change and Community Action*. London: Jessica Kingsley, 2001.
Gough, Tim. *Rebooted: Reclaiming Youth Ministry for the Long Haul: A Biblical Approach*. London: IVP, 2018.
Green, Chris. "The Incarnation and Mission." In *The Word Became Flesh: Evangelicals and the Incarnation*, edited by David Peterson, 110-151. Exeter: Paternoster, 2003.
Greig, Pete. *The Vision and the Vow*. Eastbourne: Relevant, 2004.
Griffin, Josh. "Q&A: Starting a Youth Ministry from Scratch,", *Morethandodgeball.com*, http://www.morethandodgeball.com/youth-ministry/q-a-starting-a-youth-ministry-from-scratch.html.
Griffiths, Steve. *Models for Youth Ministry*. London: SPCK, 2013.
Grenz Stanley, and Roger Olson. *Who Needs Theology?* Leicester: IVP, 1996.
Guiness, Os. *The Call*. Nashville: Word, 1998.
Handy, Charles B. *The Age of Paradox*. Harvard: Harvard Business School, 1994.
———. "Where are you on the Sigmoid Curve?" *Directors and Boards*. Fall 1994.
Hart, Roger. *Children's Participation: The Theory And Practice Of Involving Young Citizens In Community Development And Environmental Care*. Florence: UNICEF, 1997.
HASCAS, *Children and Young People's Participation in CAHMS: A Literature Review for Informed Practice*, HASCAS, 2008.
Healy, Nicholas M. "Logic of Karl Barth's Ecclesiology." *Modern Theology*, 10 no 3.1994, 254-6.
Hebblethwaite, Brian. "Incarnation." In *A Dictionary of Christian Spirituality*, edited by Gordon S. Wakefield. London: SCM, 1983, 211.
Heflin, Houston. *Youth Pastor*. Nashville: Abingdon, 2009.

Bibliography

Heneage, Kristan. "Berbatov Gains the Space to Flourish Once Again," 2nd March 2013. *CricketSoccer*. http://cricketsoccer.com/berbatov-gains-the-space-to-flourish-once-again/.

Hersch, Patricia. *A Tribe Apart: A Journey into the Heart of American Adolescence*. New York: Ballantine, 1998.

Hilborn, David, and Matt Bird. *God and the Generations*. Carlisle: Paternoster, 2002.

Hillier, Andy. "Editorial: The Erosion of Voluntary Participation." *CYPN*, (November 2008) 2.

Hughes, Bryn. *Leadership Toolkit*. Eastbourne: Kingsway, 1998.

———. *Small Group Know How*. Oxford: Monarch, 2001.

Hull, Bill. *The Complete Book of Discipleship*. USA: NavPress, 2007.

Humphrey, Edith M. "One, Holy, Catholic and Apostolic." In *Evangelical Ecclesiology: Reality or Illusion?* edited by John G. Stackhouse, 135-59. Grand Rapids: Baker, 2003.

Hybels, Bill. *Courageous Leadership*. Grand Rapids: Zondervan, 2002.

———. "Here to There." *Willow Creek Global Summit 2010*. http://www.willowcreekglobalsummit.com/downloads/here_to_there/fantastic_people/Here_to_There_-_Fantastic_People_Outline_and_Process_Tool.pdf.

Jinkins, Michael. "The 'Gift' of the Church." In *Evangelical Ecclesiology: Reality or Illusion?* edited by John G. Stackhouse, 179-209. Grand Rapids: Baker, 2003.

Justice League. Directed by Zack Snyder. California: Warner Bros, 2017.

Kageler, Len. *The Volunteer's Field Guide to Youth Ministry*. Loveland: Group, 2011.

Kandiah, Krish. "It Takes a Whole Church to Raise a Child." *Youthwork* 2 Issue 15 (March 2012) 14-6.

Kinnaman, David. *You Lost Me: Why Young Christians are Leaving the Church… And Rethinking Faith*. Grand Rapids: Baker, 2011.

Kouzes, James M. and Barry Z. Posner. *Credibility: How Leaders Gain and Lose It, Why People Demand It*. San Francisco: Jossey Bass, 1993.

Kraft, Charles. *Christianity in Culture*. New York: Orbis, 1979.

Lawrence, Rick. *Jesus Centered Youth Ministry*. Loveland: Group, 2007.

The Lego Batman Movie. Directed by Chris McKay. California: Warner Bros, 2017

Lewis, C.S. *Letters of C.S. Lewis,* ed. W.H. Lewis. New York: Harcourt Brace Jovanovich, 1966.

———. *Mere Christianity*. Glasgow: Fount, 1952.

Locke, John. "A Letter Concerning Toleration." In *On Politics and Education,* edited by John Locke, 27-8. New York: Walter J. Black, 1947.

Luft, Joseph, and Harry Ingham. *The Johari Window: A Graphic Model for Interpersonal Relations*. Los Angeles: UCLA, 1955.

Majoribanks, David, and Anna Darnell Bradley. *The Way We Are Now – The State of the UK's Relationships,* Scotland: Relate, 2017. https://www.relate.org.uk/sites/default/files/the_way_we_are_now_-_youre_not_alone.pdf

Matlock, Mark "5 Reasons the Church Needs Youth Ministry." *Youth Specialties*. 7th July 2014. www.youtube.com/watch?v=3momk_FNNLI.

Matrix Revolutions. Directed by The Wachowski Brothers, California: Warner Bros, 2003.

Maxwell, John C. *The 21 Irrefutable Laws of Leadership*. Nashville: Thomas Nelson, Inc., 1998.

Michael McGarry. *A Biblical Theology of Youth Ministry*. Nashville: Randall House, 2019.

BIBLIOGRAPHY

McGonigal, Terry. "Focusing Youth Ministry through Evangelism." In *Starting Right: Thinking theologically about youth ministry*, edited by Kenda Creasy Dean, Chap Clark and Dave Rahn, 125-6. Grand Rapids: Zondervan, 2001.

Mckiernan, Aidan. "The Problem of Batman: Is Batman a Superhero?" *HeroDistrict.com*, 11th July 2011, http://herodistrict.com/2011/07/11/the-problem-of-batman-is-batman-a-superhero-2/.

Minear, Paul Sevier. *Images of the Church in the New Testament*. Louisville: Presbyterian, 2004.

Moltmann, Jürgen. *God for a Secular Society*. London: SCM, 1999.

———. *Theology of Hope*. London: SCM, 1967.

Montefiore, C.G. *Rabbinic Literature and Gospel Teaching*. New York: Ktav, 1939.

Morris, Helen D. *Flexible Church*. London: SCM, 2019.

Nash, Robert Scott. *1 Corinthians. Smyth & Helwys Bible Commentary*. Macon: Smyth & Helwys, 2009.

Newbigin, Lesslie, *The Gospel in a Pluralist Society*. London: SPCK, 1989.

Nolland, John. *The Gospel of Matthew: A Commentary on the Greek Text*. NIGTC. Grand Rapids: W.B. Eerdmans, 2005.

Oestreicher, Mark. *Youth Ministry 3.0: A Manifesto of Where We've Been, Where We Are, and Where We Need to Go*. Grand Rapids: Youth Specialties, 2008.

Ott, Craig, and Stephen J. Strauss. *Encountering Theology of Mission*. Grand Rapids: Baker Academic, 2010.

Parsons, Rob. "Parents: Sharing the Load." *Youthwork*, (June 2011) 18-20.

Peterson, Eugene. "The Business of Making Saints." *Leadership Journal* (Spring 1997) 20-8.

Pilavachi, Mike. "The Vision: The Youth Worker." *Youthwork*, (August 2009) 24.

Rice, Wayne. *Reinventing Youth Ministry (Again)*. Downer's Grove: IVP, 2010.

Root, Andrew. *Revisiting Relational Youth Ministry*. Downers Grove: IVP, 2007.

———. "The Incarnation, Place-sharing, and Youth Ministry: Experiencing the Transcendence of God." *The Journal of Youth Ministry* 12(1) (2013) 23.

Root Andy, and Kenda Creasy Dean. *The Theological Turn in Youth Ministry*. Downers Grove: IVP, 2011.

Santrock, J.W. *Adolescence*. 4th ed. Iowa: William C Brown, 1990.

Saunders, Martin. *Youth Work From Scratch*. Oxford: Monarch, 2013.

Savage, Sara, Sylvia Collins-Mayo, and Bob Mayo. *Making Sense of Generation Y*. London: Church House, 2006.

Senter III, Mark H. and Warren S. Benson. *The Complete Book of Youth Ministry*. Chicago: Moody Press, 1987.

Smith, Mark K. *Developing Youth Work: Informal Education, Mutual Aid and Popular Practice*. OUP, 1988.

Smith, Mark K. Naomi Stanton, and Tom Wylie, eds. *Youth Work and Faith: Debates, Delights and Dilemmas*. Lyme Regis: Russell House, 2013.

Stanley, Andy. "Get it done Leadership." *Leadership*. Spring (2006) 26-32.

Stapleton, Alan. "Residential Disillusion?" *Core Christian Residential Experiences*. Issue 1 (February 2011) 12.

Sweet, Leonard. *Viral*. Colorado: WaterPress, 2012.

Swindoll, Charles R. *Insights on Luke*. Grand Rapids: Zondervan, 2012.

Thiselton, Anthony C. *The First Epistle to the Corinthians: a commentary on the Greek text*. NIGTC. Grand Rapids: W.B. Eerdmans, 2000.

Bibliography

Tidball, Derek. *Skilful Shepherds*. Leicester: IVP, 1986.

Voas, David, and Laura Watt. "Numerical change in church attendance: National, local and individual factors." *The Church Growth Research Programme Report on Strands 1 & 2*, (2014).

Walker, J. *Testing Fresh Expressions*. Abingdon: Routledge, 2014.

Ward, Pete. *God at the Mall*. Baker Academic, 1998.

———. *Growing up evangelical*. London: SPCK, 1996.

———. *Youthwork and the Mission of God*. London: SPCK, 1997.

Watson, David. *I Believe in the Church*. London: Hodder & Stoughton, 1978.

White, David. "The Social Construction of Adolescence." In *Awakening Youth Discipleship: Christian Resistance in a Consumer Culture*. Edited by Brian J. Mahan, Michael Warren and David F. White. 3-19. Eugene: Cascade, 2008.

Wyn, J., and R. White. *Rethinking Youth*. London: SAGE, 1997.

Woodall, Trinny, and Susannah Constantine. *The Body Shape Bible*. London: Weidenfeld & Nicolson, 2007.

Woods, Rod. *Freed to Lead: How Your Identity in Christ can Transform any Leadership Role*. Oxford: Monarch, 2016.

Yaconelli, Mike. *Getting Fired for the Glory of God*. Grand Rapids: Zondervan, 2008.

Young, Terry. *After the Fishermen: How Did Jesus Train His Disciples*. Carlisle: Paternoster, 2004.

www.ingramcontent.com/pod-product-compliance
Lightning Source LLC
Chambersburg PA
CBHW050822160426
43192CB00010B/1857